HOW
TO ENJOY
THEATRE

HOW
TO ENJOY
THEATRE

Philip Cook

Series Editor Melvyn Bragg

PIATKUS

To Sue

For every reason . . .

Frontispiece: A rare Goldoni play, *The Impresario from Smyrna,* translated and directed by Robert David MacDonald at the Glasgow Citizens' Theatre, January 1983. Carlo Goldoni (1707–93), the Italian comic dramatist, is best known to British audiences for his *The Servant of Two Masters.*

© 1983 Philip Cook

First published in 1983 by Judy Piatkus (Publishers) Limited of Loughton, Essex

British Library Cataloguing in Publication Data

Cook, Philip
   How to enjoy theatre.—(Melvyn Bragg's arts series)
   1. Theatre
   I. Title   II. Series
   792   PN2037

   ISBN 0-86188-142-7

Designed by Zena Flax

Typeset by Phoenix Photosetting, Chatham, Kent
Printed and bound by Mackays of Chatham Ltd

contents

A scene from the National Theatre production of *Plenty* by David Hare.

introduction

It is a commonplace but nonetheless remarkable fact that certain arts constantly flourish in particular countries. Not that those countries have the monopoly, or are necessarily always in the forefront, but the tradition holds. Germany is noted for a multi-royal flush of opera houses; Russia for ballet schools and ballet companies; America for the twentieth-century Arts – movies, jazz, rock, pop, dance; Ireland for men of letters; England for the theatre. It is, I think, very fine that the greatest Englishman should have been not a king nor a warrior, not a statesman nor a philosopher, but William Shakespeare: playwright.

This book attempts – in the widest possible fashion – to describe the vast and varied terrain of drama. The determination to be both comprehensive and accessible makes this both a guidebook for those who have an interest but little knowledge, and a handbook for those whose knowledge might need support. The complication and diffusion of theatrical history and practices must have made it especially difficult to decant into one volume. But Philip

Cook's undisguised enthusiasm and wide interest manages to make his whirlwind tour both entertaining and, especially in the historical section, most succinctly useful.

Despite repeated threats of demise, the theatre in Britain in this last quarter of the twentieth century must be considered to be in fairly good shape. At the grass-roots there are about 1,000,000 people who take part in amateur theatricals. There is probably not a village, market town or borough in the country which does not have its drama group. This general interest is nourished in the schools where a more intelligent awareness of the values of the theatre has encouraged many education authorities to permit and aid the development of drama on the syllabus; regular plays are now an established pride of many schools, which, no more than a generation ago, struggled to put on a hacked-down version of a Shakespeare comedy once every winter.

Again in the general arena, radio and television have been an immense stimulus to drama. BBC Radio's drama department is the single biggest commissioner of new plays in the world. A great number of our leading playwrights began in the bowels of that beached submarine in Portland Place, Broadcasting House. The radio, moreover, was and remains catholic in its choice of plays. Classics are revived, popular old favourites re-vamped and re-written, soap operas unblushingly purveyed, tentative and difficult new writers sought out, novels adapted; in short the variousness of the public's involvement in drama is reflected, institutionalised and thus made reputable by BBC Radio. There is no sense from radio that 'The Theatre' is available only to a certain and limited group of fortunate initiates.

This tradition has been carried over into television. Once again, it is the range, the commitment and the skills involved across the spectrum which are impressive. They both stimulate and reinforce diversity. Whether it is for horror-stories, domestic trials, cops-and-robbers, mysteries and murders, the tradition of naturalism which has had such a powerful influence on contemporary dramatists, or the tradition of Shakespeare which is kept vivid even on the small television screen – the British television public is offered a great variety of drama. It responds well. The most popular television programmes are drama serials; the most enjoyed television programmes are dramatic adaptations of favoured novels; and the most important television programmes – in my view – over the last twenty-five years, have been original television plays. Plays by David Mercer, Harold Pinter, Tom Stoppard, John Osborne, Alan Bennett, Alan Bleasdale, Dennis Potter, Stephen Poliakoff, John Allen – and many others – have brought British television audiences to their feet in sympathy or in fury again and again.

It is on this foundation – a well developed do-it-yourself involvement in amateur theatre and a well endowed representation of the best of both classical and contemporary drama in the most popular media – that the substantial interest in the theatre in this country rests.

Its glory, many believe, still rests on the stage. With the great companies – the Royal Shakespeare Company and the National Theatre; the Fringe and writers' theatres – the Royal Court, the Bush, the King's Head, the Half-Moon; the successful theatres outside London – the Glasgow Citizens', the Nottingham Playhouse, the Bristol Old Vic; and the West End, still with more than forty theatres, forever saving itself in the final reel. Last year (1982) about 300 plays opened in London: that figure does not allow for the several plays which had already been on for a year or more. Three hundred. As many as in almost all the other European capitals combined. In America moreover, in the same year, the Brits stormed Broadway with the Royal Shakespeare's *Nicholas Nickleby*, a nine-hour Dickensian epic which bit the big apple to the core; *Cats*, the musical which began with a handful of poems by an American Anglophile High Anglican exile; *Amadeus*, from the original National Theatre production; and plays by Pinter, Cecil Taylor, Caryl Churchill, David Hare, and so it went on. Contemporary British plays can be seen in most German cities; British directors, designers and stage technicians swarm all over the world fixing productions in one country or another; the conclusion must be that the British theatre is up and kicking.

The foundation for this success is the Arts Council's £23 million grant coupled with the ingenuity of West End managements to winkle commercial success from a mixture of the tried and the entirely new. Oddly enough, it is the West End managements which have been at a recent disadvantage – with VAT, transport problems and subsidised competition. But the Theatre Investment Fund, the work of the Society of West End Theatres (SWET), and the realisation that good plays, well produced, still bring in the audiences combine to give persistent evidence that there is life yet in the West End.

At the present time we live in a country in which actors such as Olivier, Gielgud, Richardson, McKellen, Howard, Kingsley, Conti, Janet Suzman, Felicity Kendal, Peggy Ashcroft and Suzanne Bertish are but the tip of a mass of talent; a theatre which sustains writers such as Pinter, Stoppard, Frayn, Nichols, Churchill, Gems – and that in true cliché style is to mention but a few; which nourishes great companies and very fine production teams, builds new theatres and somehow keeps intact the old. It may not be the best of times but it seems to me far from being the worst of times. Curtain up, then, on this look at the drama behind the stage.

Melvyn Bragg
19th April, 1983

1

WHAT
IS
THEATRE?

To enjoy a play you need neither special knowledge nor a special attitude; your presence alone is required – the magic of theatre will do the rest.

The tradition of theatre is a long one going back well over 2,500 years. Over the centuries the nature of drama and the manner of its presentation have changed considerably; the theatre has adapted and responded to changing times and sentiments. It has moved from ritual to easy naturalism, from religious fervour to bawdy entertainment, from being an outdoor activity to an indoor one, from periods of rare and occasional performance to twice-nightly ones. It has survived decades of outright condemnation and total prohibition – and continues to survive. In fact theatre today is going through one of its most striking periods of adaptability, and its forms and activities are more varied and widespread than they have ever been.

Theatre has always been a spirited affair, its live flesh-and-blood performers generating imaginative responses in its audience and occasionally provoking the unexpected. Take for instance the story told of a performance in Ancient Greece, where the appearance of actors in a particular scene was so horrifying that pregnant women in the audience miscarried. It is said too that in Ancient Rome certain performances which called for violence and death were gruesomely realistic; convicted criminals were introduced into the cast, and in the course of the action summarily dispatched!

Modern theatre is less sensational, but it can still provide headline news, as it did when actors and actresses bared their all in the first full frontal nudity shows, *Hair* and *Oh! Calcutta,* in the 1960s. Nudity and sex on stage are still controversial issues, as witness the prosecution in 1980 of a director of the National Theatre over their production of Howard Brenton's *The Romans in Britain.* Riots in theatres due to the actions of inconsiderate managements or the short-comings of plays and players were not uncommon throughout the eighteenth and nineteenth centuries; notable among them were the Old Price Riots at Covent Garden Theatre in 1809, which continued unabated at every performance for sixty-seven nights. (The theatre, which had burned down the previous year, had been reopened with increased admission charges to offset the cost of the new building. Patrons resented the higher prices – caring little for the new design of the theatre – and also objected to the employment of large numbers of Italian artistes.) As recently as the early decades of this century, audiences at the Abbey Theatre in Dublin rioted over certain plays by their own countrymen, J. M. Synge and Sean O'Casey.

Clearly, theatre is a powerful medium. It is capable of influencing the thought and feeling of its audience to a remarkable degree, usually through its stock-in-trade of laughter and tears. It can make you laugh and cry or provide you with pure escapism. It can also be altogether more serious – it can delight the mind and engage the intellect. Going to the theatre is a tonic. As the curtain goes up, the mundane world recedes and an imaginary one takes over. Perhaps theatre does not so much take you out of yourself as take you *into* yourself, enabling you to discover new frontiers within your mind, opening up hitherto unexplored territories, engaging your attention on unfamiliar issues.

The great strength and special attraction of the theatre

is its immediacy; it is *live* entertainment. In a theatre you are watching a performance that is taking place in front of you, now. And such performances – though the audience are unaware of it – are subtly responding to the mood of that audience, helping them to get the most out of the evening's entertainment. Live theatre indulges its audience over passages that are going down well, and moves on swiftly when it senses disinterest. Film and television have no such facility: the performance is fixed.

Another aspect of theatre-going which can never be experienced at home in front of a television set is the corporate sense of wellbeing and togetherness that develops in a theatre audience. Just before the play begins, when the lights in the auditorium dim and there is a brief pause, the audience becomes 'one'. They stop chatting and settle down expectantly; before this moment they were hundreds of individuals or couples, but now a sense of unity is created which is strengthened as the performance proceeds. They laugh together, hold their breath together, respond together. This in turn produces a feeling of belonging, of relaxation and mutual wellbeing, like members of an exclusive club all known to each other and privileged to witness something rather special. This atmosphere is especially noticeable at a successful comedy, when an audience will be particularly relaxed and happy, while at a serious play their attentiveness is increased and concentration intensified. After a performance, perfect strangers will talk to each other and those who went alone to the theatre feel less alone. A shared experience has proved salutary, and quite apart from what the members of the audience have derived from the play itself, they have benefited from the mere experiencing of it in the company of other people.

This is what theatre is all about – communicating and stimulating a response, whether it be to laugh, to cry or to think. Theatre is particularly suited to achieve this end since it deals with most of the senses. In a theatre you see, hear and understand, and you can almost taste and smell the atmosphere as well.

An all-out effort by a playwright to engage the senses results in what is called total theatre. *The Royal Hunt of the*

Sun (1964) by Peter Shaffer is a fine example. Its subject matter alone is exotic enough – the sixteenth-century conquest of the Incas of Peru by the Spanish Conquistadores. Translated into visual and aural terms on stage it is stunning. The costumes and settings, the drumming and chanting and the essence of all drama – conflict – make an amazing piece of total theatre.

But a play can be powerful using only the simplest of settings (drapes and a couple of benches), naturalistic acting and ordinary everyday clothes – provided the theme is riveting enough. It certainly is in *Children of a Lesser God* by Mark Medoff, presented in 1981 at the Mermaid Theatre from which it quickly transferred into the West End for a long run. This play has a highly unlikely theme, that of the deaf and dumb, and, even more remarkable, it calls for a leading lady who speaks not a single word throughout the play. In fact in the London production this central role was played by a deaf and dumb actress – something which you might think an impossibility in the theatre, but which in the event produced a performance of tremendous pathos and power. The play takes place in a school of speech therapy and shows the emotional relationship which develops between a sympathetic, non-handicapped male teacher and a deaf and dumb female employee. Much of the 'dialogue' of the play is conveyed through sign language, translated by the teacher, but at the centre of the play are the conflict and frustration experienced by the deaf and dumb girl. On the face of it both the topic and its simple staging might be thought to lack appeal, but the play won many awards for both acting and writing and has proven a very powerful piece of theatre indeed.

These two productions demonstrate the enormous range of the theatre and its ability to stimulate and entertain. It is the ability of theatre simultaneously to stimulate thought and to entertain which has made it such a lasting art form. While there is still a place and indeed a need for simple

Opposite: *The Royal Hunt of the Sun* by Peter Shaffer – an excellent example of total theatre.

popular entertainment – the farce, the outrageous comedy, the spectacular musical, something to while away a couple of hours pleasantly and send you back into the world with your batteries recharged – theatre is effective in other ways. It has the power to shock, to provoke, to stimulate, to enlighten and to educate.

Plays can be deliberately contrived to make an audience question previously accepted viewpoints; to shake them out of too cosy assumptions; to raise issues that they would prefer to forget about; to suggest that old ways of doing things need to be rethought. The plight of the homeless, the stigma of mental illness, and the taking of children into care, are a few topics that have recently been tackled. The questioning nature of theatre can also open up for discussion subjects previously thought too delicate or taboo. The aim of the playwright in all these cases has been not to suggest solutions, but to make the public more aware, and to provoke discussion in the hope that better solutions than existing ones may be found. By presenting problems in a dramatised way an audience can be confronted with the question 'What would you have done in similar circumstances?'

Theatre therefore can have a positive role to play in society over and above that of purveying popular entertainment. It can question, inform, expose or coax an audience to respond actively to any number of topics and situations. Occasionally it goes beyond coaxing and positively affronts its audience, using shock tactics to ensure that no one remains unmoved. The Royal Shakespeare Company, for instance, in a production called *US*, deliberately burnt on stage a fragile and beautiful butterfly to make a point (though they swore later that it was not a real butterfly). Another play, by a different company, featured a bowl of goldfish. The goldfish were swallowed alive by an actor and the water from the bowl sloshed at the audience. Other shock tactics have been to insult the audience verbally and even physically to man-handle a few of them. It is what is known as 'getting a response'. Such practices are usually the preserve of fringe or experimental theatre groups – they are unlikely to occur in mainstream theatre.

Theatre, then, comes in many guises. It can be

Commitments by Dusty Hughes at the Bush Theatre – one of London's highly successful pub theatres. *Duet for One* which had a rave West End run originated at the Bush.

magically beautiful or violently cruel, it can be thrilling or merely charming, stimulating or reassuring, purely for pleasure or something to make you think – there is something for everyone. One of the greatest excitements of going to the theatre today is that you never know quite what to expect – there is such a diversity of subject matter and so many forms of presentation. But however it comes, it is *live,* and not a second-hand effect; it is something to be *experienced.*

When you are watching a good production in the theatre you experience what is technically known as the 'willing suspension of disbelief'. You know that the people on the stage acting out the play are actors and not really the characters they say they are, and that you are sitting in a theatre watching a performance of a play. Yet somehow, such is the effect created that you gradually forget all that and become drawn into the world of the play. You believe for the time being, however fleetingly, that what is happening on stage is actually taking place; the strength of the actors' 'make believe' has made it as 'real' to you as it obviously is for them.

But the art of theatre is not simply to act out a story and to make it appear real – more importantly, it is to show you *how* and *why* it happened the way it did. It does not simply tell a story – it makes you *feel* it, it *shows* you. It can therefore be a moving, emotional experience.

Today, theatres are trying to attract larger audiences and to appeal to a wider section of the community. Theatre buildings have taken on a whole new image. At one time they were only open in the evenings, or for the occasional matinee performance, but now theatres, especially the modern regional repertory theatres, have become 'social centres'. Open to everyone from mid-morning until late evening, they are places to enjoy. They house exhibitions and art shows, have bars, bookstalls and buffets, and most larger ones have restaurants. At weekends, supplementary activities such as a craft fair or a film show increase the use of the building and during the week there may be lunchtime talks or short recitals. So get used to the idea of dropping in at your local theatre. If you have not yet seen a performance there, these activities provide the ideal opportunity for you to get to know the building and see what plays are due to be presented.

Basically there are two sorts of theatre in Britain today: first commercial, and second sponsored and subsidised. Commercial theatre, as its name implies, exists to make money. To this end commercial theatre usually chooses plays in the light entertainment bracket, such as comedy, farce, thrillers and musicals, and presents 'straight' plays (often revivals of past successes) featuring star casts and person-alities. London has recently seen the legendary Hollywood film star Elizabeth Taylor in a revival of *The Little Foxes* by Lillian Hellman.

Sponsored and subsidised theatre, on the other hand, are heavily supported by such funding bodies as the Arts Council, local authorities, large business firms, and cultural organisations. Organisations like the Goethe Institute, for instance, will provide grants to subsidise companies presenting the work of German playwrights. Major banks and insurance companies will sponsor specific productions in return for advertising; it is considered beneficial for their public image to be associated with the arts. The distinction between sponsorship and subsidy is best expressed in the Arts Council's publication *Arts in Action*: 'Patronage [subsidy] is a charitable gesture with no expectation of a return; sponsorship is a commercial transaction from which the sponsor expects a good return in publicity and advertising value.' The major funding body for subsidised theatre is, of course, the Arts Council of Great Britain, which distributes monies provided by the government to promote the arts generally. In the 1981–82 season, the Arts Council distributed £23 million to theatrical companies throughout Britain.

Such theatrical companies are technically known as non-profit-distributing companies, for any profit made by them has to be ploughed back. The policy of sponsored and subsidised theatre is therefore much broader than that of commercial theatre, since the choice of play is not determined solely by box office potential. New plays, the classics, experimental work and so on can all be presented, in addition to popular entertainment.

In London, commercial theatre predominates; in the regions it is almost wholly subsidised theatre. Subsidised theatre usually operates with a more or less permanent company engaged for a season and performing several plays, whereas commercial theatre works on a one-off principle, generally assembling a different company for each production. Fringe and alternative theatre is usually subsidised theatre; either funded by the Arts Council and so on, or as a result of direct appeal to patrons and anyone who might be persuaded to contribute.

The scale and standard of production achieved in both commercial and subsidised theatre depends largely on the finance available, which controls such things as the size of the theatre and the company employed, as well as the status of the artistic director and designers. The theatre has to cut its suit according to its cloth. Lavish productions of costume dramas and the classics can rarely be mounted nowadays except by the National Theatre Company and the Royal Shakespeare Company, and perhaps more infrequently by a wealthy commercial company.

2

GOING
TO A
PLAY

Having decided to see a play, should you prepare yourself beforehand? If so, in what way? Is it nececessary to have read the play?

The answer to the last question is a categorical no! Plays are not novels or poems, but were designed and written in dramatic terms for presentation in a theatre. The text of a play is a blueprint requiring the skills of a director, designer, actors and stage-hands to bring it to life on-stage. Only an experienced, practised eye can read a text and visualise its total impact in a theatre. Study the text *afterwards* by all means, but first see it where it was designed to be experienced, in the theatre.

For the first-time viewer of plays like Ibsen's *Hedda Gabler* or Chekhov's *The Seagull* it would be a distinct disadvantage to know what is going to happen to the central characters; however, because of the profound nature and complexity of most classic plays, a study of the text after you have seen a performance will be helpful. No single visit to a production of, say, one of Shakespeare's major tragedies can possibly convey all that it has to offer.

It is sensible to check in advance the genre, or the kind of play you are to see. Is it comedy, tragedy, farce, melodrama, etc? Otherwise you may find a play heavy and serious when what you really wanted was something light and amusing. A fine play and production, however, generate their own interest and will probably win you over irrespective of your mood. Serious plays are not absolutely devoid of humour, and vice versa. For instance, a play set in a hospital ward and concerning a gifted young artist afflicted with near-total paralysis might not sound an ideal subject for an evening's entertainment. But *Whose Life Is It Anyway?* by Brian Clark, one of the most outstandingly successful recent new plays, was written so brilliantly and with such wit that few people found it morbid. No matter in what mood people arrived to see this play, it certainly captured their attention.

The publicity matter, especially for a new play, will usually indicate the kind of play it is – 'the craziest comedy ever . . .' or 'the wickedest farce of all time . . .' or 'the most serious play of the decade. . . .' If it is described simply as 'a play', it is more likely to be serious than comic. Most playwrights stick to familiar ground and do not switch from tragedy to zany farce or comedy; a new play by Alan Ayckbourn is most likely to be another light domestic comedy; Tom Stoppard deals in witty intellectual games; while Edward Bond is a serious politically committed writer. Past playwrights are more readily categorised; Strindberg wrote no comedies, Molière no tragedies; Chekhov's plays are full of pathos, Oscar Wilde's of witty conceits.

Discovering whether the play you intend seeing is of an unusual or specific nature – whether it is a period play, for instance, and belongs to a broad historic or national group, such as Greek tragedy, French neo-classical drama, English medieval drama or Italian *commedia dell'arte* – will alert you to expect a special kind of performance, quite unlike modern contemporary drama. It will also prevent you from ending up bemused by the play's strange structure, treatment or subject matter, and from falling into the trap of condemning a play because it is unlike a modern play. The National Theatre's 1981 production of *The Oresteia* by Aeschylus is a case in point. Aware that the play is a Greek tragedy – or, to be

precise, three plays in one – the audience were prepared for the use of masks, a chorus, an all-male cast, little action and dialogue of a very stylised kind.

Questions can be answered by the theatre box office and by critics' reviews. It is the critic's job not only to assess the actors' performances and the effectiveness of the production, but also to comment on matters of genre and to locate the play in its period.

When you go to a performance you should be aware that every single thing you see and hear on stage has been carefully pre-planned – the colour of a particular dress, the exact moment at which a cigarette is lit or a drink taken, and whether a character stands or sits. Nothing happens by chance.

All this planning has a dramatic purpose. Take costume for instance. What an actor wears tells you immediately something about the character he is playing – whether he is rich or poor, unfashionable or trendy, a member of a particular profession, and so on. But it also tells you something about his disposition – that he is careless or precise, reserved or outgoing. And all this is clear to you, the audience, long before the character has spoken a word.

The setting of the play – the scenery and what the stage looks like – can also be very informative. Apart from the obvious manner in which the furniture and decor will tell you the period and location of the play, the way the scenery is painted and the type of object placed on-stage will indicate something further. If the setting is the interior of a Gothic castle, but painted unrealistically with lots of heavily lined shadows and cross-hatchings, giving a flat look and not one of three-dimensional realism, then you can safely assume that the play is going to be a light-hearted one. If the play were meant to be taken more seriously, the setting would be painted more naturalistically.

Opposite: Orestes and the Chorus from Part III of Aeschylus' trilogy *The Oresteia,* in Peter Hall's prestigous production at the National Theatre, November 1981.

If the setting is totally non-realistic, composed of symbolic forms that merely indicate a location but offer no specific details, then you may expect the dialogue and action of the play to be similarly symbolic and unnaturalistic. Generally speaking, the mood created by the stage setting always conveys and reinforces the mood of the play. A light-hearted comedy would not show to its best advantage if played against a dark, heavy, gloomy set. Similarly a tragic play such as *King Lear* would have its impact lessened if presented in a light, open setting brightly lit in sunshine yellow.

If the setting is a non-naturalistic one, composed of strange shapes and colours, it is important not to dismiss it as abstract or trendy but to analyse it for what it might convey. Deliberately designed symbolic settings can have immense significance and contribute a powerful dimension to a play. *Macbeth,* for instance, played against a dark, shadowy background with the stage carpeted in blood-red, suggests the play's intrinsic action of dark deeds and blood-letting. A play set against a background of huge megalithic stones can suggest the puniness of man and the immensity of time. An acting area defined by a circle (clearly non-naturalistic) can suggest many things – a global significance, the ring of life, a trap-like circular environment, and so on. A play with an almost bare stage can suggest symbolic action applicable to *all* time and space and unconfined to any particular time or place. A steel-grey setting unrelieved by other colours, full of sharp angles and hard edges, can convey a severely oppressive feeling – a warlike atmosphere. The scope of scenic design to enhance a play's effect is enormous. Even before the action starts, the setting, like costume, informs an audience in general terms about what is likely to follow.

Stage lighting is also important in a production, though paradoxically the more effective it is the less it draws attention to itself. The basic – though not the sole – purpose of stage lighting is to illuminate the actors and the stage and to inform an audience of such obvious matters as daylight, moonlight, tropical or arctic conditions. With the aid of filters, stage lighting can produce an effect of warmth or cold and can contribute enormously to the emotional temperature of a scene. Intensity of light, for instance, can heighten a scene's

Ian McKellen as Macbeth consults the witches in the RSC's much
acclaimed studio production at The Other Place,
Stratford-upon-Avon, 1976.

effectiveness, while dim lighting full of shade and shadows can create a feeling of foreboding or terror: the range of effects is infinite. Stage lighting is seldom static, and although an audience may well not notice it, the lighting operator is continually changing the balance of light and shade throughout a show; in the hands of a good director and lighting designer it can be a most effective tool.

In the old days, the convention of soliloquies and the stage aside was used to tell the audience what a character was thinking in such a way that the rest of the cast on stage were not supposed to overhear. Today, special lighting effects do the job much better. A recent production of Shakespeare's *The Winter's Tale* used this kind of effect in the opening scene of the play, in which King Leontes is filled with sudden jealousy at the attention his wife is receiving from an old and hitherto well-loved friend. The king has several long speeches (asides) which are mixed in with the rest of the cast's conversation. These speeches, which are really only the rumblings of his subconscious mind, must be delivered without upsetting the rest of the scene, which proceeds naturally. As Leontes spoke of his wildest fears that he was being cuckolded, he was sharply lit while the rest of the cast went into shadow. Normal lighting was resumed as the speech reverted to normal conversation. Such an effect was more direct and exciting than the stage aside – time appeared to stand still for a moment.

It is also helpful to be aware of the patterns of stage grouping made by the actors on-stage. This is a highly skilled business, which is the province of the director. It is his job to ensure that the cast are displayed on-stage to the best advantage, and that in their moves across the stage they do not conceal or bump into each other! It is often not as easy as it looks, especially with a dozen or more people on a small stage filled with furniture and other objects.

The aim of good grouping is to ensure that everyone is seen without being 'masked' (the technical term indicating that an actor is hidden behind another or is obscured by, say, a portion of the set), that they are pleasingly distributed on-stage (not all facing front in a single straight line) and that dramatic confrontations or special relationships between various members of the cast are reflected in the grouping itself. For instance, if a scene contains one rebel towards whom all the other characters on-stage are antagonistic, a good director will isolate that individual and arrange the rest of the cast so that the resulting stage picture is of one facing many. In a duologue, the positioning of the two actors can contribute an extra dimension to the scene. For example, if the two characters are arguing more and more angrily, then the closer they are to each other the more powerfully will the argument be felt by the audience. Conversely, two people locked in a discussion but speaking to each other from opposite sides of a room will indicate that they are symbolically as well as physically apart. A character at an upper or higher stage level than another will dominate that person; an actor standing in the centre of the stage will be in a more commanding position than one who is upstage in a corner.

There are certain features about the positioning of actors on-stage which over the centuries have proved effective and which always work; these have become the unwritten laws on-stage and are only broken in special circumstances. Learning to interpret stage pictures and groupings will help you enjoy the more subtle points of a production.

Having seen a play, do not be tempted to take it entirely at its face value. Metaphor and allegory are potent weapons in the hands of a playwright. *The Crucible* by Arthur Miller, for instance, appears at first sight to be a straightforward account of witch-hunting in Salem, Massachusetts in the seventeenth century. As an account of those times it is dramatically very satisfying – it tells a story and is completely self-contained. But the play's significance goes far beyond a mere historical representation. It is an allegory of another form of witch-hunting that shattered America in the early 1950s – the fierce denunciations of 'anti-American' activities led by Senator McCarthy. Read in this light, the play takes on altogether richer and more sinister connotations. *The Kitchen* by Arnold Wesker, set entirely in the kitchen of a London restaurant, certainly details the stresses and strains which occur at such an establishment, but the kitchen is also meant to be interpreted as a microcosm of the world.

Edward Albee's smash-hit play *Who's Afraid of*

Virginia Woolf? is not at all concerned with the celebrated English novelist of that name, and has far more significance than a tale of four people coming back for drinks after an evening out. Again, the playwright is using allegory, this time to comment on the 'American Dream'. Clues to such an interpretation start with the names of the four characters; George and Martha (significantly the christian names of a past US President and his wife) and Honey and Nick. Honey, a timorous young wife, is symbolically the sickly sweet child who has scarcely left her spoonfed nursery, utterly dependent on her virile young husband, who is aptly named Nick – for it is the devil of his sexual attraction for Martha which precipitates quarrels and recriminations that last into the small hours of the morning before the dawn of truth is faced. The names of characters in plays can often prove fruitful when you are seeking an interpretation. The playwrights of the past went about it quite blatantly, using names such as Mr Petulant, Squire Sullen, Sir Novelty Fashion, Zeal-of-the-Land-Busy and, perhaps the most famous of them all, Mrs Malaprop, who was constantly speaking 'malapropisms' such as 'allegories on the banks of the Nile'.

Certain plays are so strange that they are clearly not meant to be taken literally. In Samuel Beckett's play *End Game,* for instance, a man and wife suddenly appear from within dustbins, and remain inside them throughout the play with only their heads and shoulders visible. No explanation is given in the play, which contains several other unexplained oddities; the audience are required to work it all out for themselves. Here, the playwright is making a point visually: dustbins are refuse containers, in which rubbish or something which has reached the end of its useful life is dumped. The playwright is asking us to see this interpretative link, suggesting that these people, too, have perhaps come to the end of their useful lives, or are unwanted, or are being disposed of. This play is an extreme example, but in serious plays you should always be alert for metaphor and allegory and be prepared to look beyond mere surface values.

When you have settled down to regular theatre-going, you will start appreciating the finer points of acting. Great performances are one of the bonuses of watching plays – you may be there on the night when everyone is on top of their form and when everything works better than it has ever done. The result is an overwhelming experience. Such occasions are unforgettable – 'the imperishable moments' which send a shiver down your spine and make your hair stand on end – Laurence Olivier as Othello, killing himself after he has strangled his wife, realising all too late that he has been duped and has made a terrible, terrible mistake . . . Vanessa Redgrave as a radiant Rosalind in *As You Like It,* crowning a scintillating performance throughout the play by a sparkling delivery of the epilogue . . . these are a couple of my 'imperishable moments'. As you see more and more productions, especially of the same play, you will take increasing pleasure in comparing actors' performances and in anticipating eagerly how certain lines or speeches will be dealt with. It is true that the more you know about theatre, the greater will be your enjoyment.

being informed

It is not difficult to know what theatrical activity is available at any time. Subsidised theatres display details of their own productions and also those of other theatres and theatre-groups in the area. Regional Arts Associations compile and circulate an Arts Newspaper which is available at theatres in the area. Local libraries display publicity material and hold copies of local newspapers.

For regular information about productions at your local theatre ask to be put on their mailing list. It is also useful to be on the mailing list of the National Theatre and the Royal Shakespeare Company, even if you do not live close to London or Stratford-upon-Avon; this way you will be aware of their major productions and touring schedules.

The monthly magazine *Plays and Players* is an excellent publication for anyone interested in the theatre. *The Stage,* the profession's weekly newspaper, is also very readable and will keep you informed of current shows and developments throughout Britain (as well as giving you all the show-biz gossip). The British Theatre Association (formerly British Drama League) publishes a quarterly review *Drama* which, although primarily concerned with amateur theatre, has now widened its scope to include professional theatre news and comment. And for the really keen theatre-goer who wants to be well informed about serious drama world-wide there are the publications *Theatre Quarterly*, *Theatre International* and *Play Bulletin.*

For those interested in London theatre there is the *London Theatre Record.* This fortnightly publication includes all previously published critical reviews of all London shows, together with information and comment on forthcoming productions. The Society of West End Theatres publishes fortnightly a *London Theatre Guide,* which again is useful if you live near London.

Going to the theatre does not have to be expensive. Concessions of various kinds exist to make theatre-going both cheaper and easier. For example, seats are cheaper at preview performances, at matinees and often at evening performances on Mondays to Thursdays. Senior citizens and students almost always qualify for price reductions, and all theatres offer reduced prices for party bookings (and anyone can make up a party).

Some theatres in the regions operate discount card schemes or offer season tickets, and both systems result in cheaper tickets. One of the latest schemes is known as stand-by – tickets which are unsold immediately before a performance are sold at cut-price rates. In London, the Leicester Square ticket booth has seats available for a large number of West End theatres on the day of performance – tickets are half the normal price plus a small service charge.

To help with travel costs, regional Arts Associations (in association with the Arts Council) will offer travel subsidies for parties of ten or more who wish to visit a theatre in the region. There is also a commercial concern called Theatre Rail Club which arranges discounts on theatre-rail package deals for over twenty London theatres; trips are arranged by rail for groups from all over Britain and these are always cheaper – and often much more convenient – than if you were to make your own booking. The many theatre clubs and arts associations up and down the country make regular visits to theatres and these often include backstage tours and lectures.

It is worth mentioning that special facilities exist in many theatres to accommodate handicapped people, especially those in wheelchairs or who are slightly hard of hearing. There is no reason why anyone so disadvantaged should feel that theatre-going is denied them. The box office will advise what arrangements are available, such as hearing aids, special entrances for the disabled, the availability of lifts, wheelchair spaces in the auditorium and seats for escorts.

Most regional theatre companies value their regular audience and actively encourage the interest of their patrons in the company's activities by creating a 'Friends of the theatre' association. The 'Friends' can meet the actors off-stage, attend talks on the various productions, visit backstage, and generally become more involved with the work of the company. It all helps to cement links between the audience and the theatre company – of benefit to public and box office alike.

3

THE
ACTOR

---

the actor's changing status

'He spoke all his words distinctly half as loud again as the others – anyone may see he is an actor' – such might have been the hallmark of the Victorian performer; but times have changed, and the only response to that kind of acting today would be a cry of 'Ham!' Acting styles change with theatre buildings, but what has not altered is the basis of all acting, creating and presenting a character other than oneself. How it is achieved depends on the society and conventions of the time, but the effectiveness and power of such a creation has been recognised since the dawn of time – acting is as old as man himself.

Acting is imitation or mimicry, and was probably first consciously used by primitive man as an aid to hunting – dressing up in antlers, skins or feathers and aping his prey so as to get close enough for a kill. But primitive societies lived in communities worshipping spirits and other deities, and their priests quickly learnt the art and usefulness of putting on a mask and costume and adopting a strange voice and impressive actions (which later became ritual dances) in order to imitate a god (see Chapter 5). Even today, especially in Africa and the Far East, religious practices produce some highly theatrical performances.

So engrained in the history of mankind is this use of mimicry that our everyday language reflects it. We speak of 'playing the fool', 'putting on an act', 'playing to the gallery' and so on. Shakespeare goes further than this in *As You Like It:* 'All the world's a stage,' he remarks, in which (to paraphrase) the men and women are merely players having their exits and their entrances, and 'one man in his time plays many parts'.

It is not surprising that in Antiquity people who were very good at 'putting on an act' (especially in the service of religion) began to specialise in this activity, which gradually developed into a recognised profession carrying the official status of 'actor'. In Ancient Greece, by the sixth and fifth centuries BC acting had developed into an elaborate art form, and eminent actors were as popular and celebrated as today's television personalities. On occasions they were even employed at state functions to deliver special orations, and in time of war often served as their country's ambassadors.

Since then, the actor's status has fluctuated, ranging from that of 'rogue and vagabond' to respected peer of the realm. From his high standing in Classical Greece the actor, along with drama, declined in Ancient Rome; the profession, no longer held in esteem, was practised only by slaves and bondsmen. Centuries later the medieval Church revived an interest in theatrical activity within the ritual of services, but it was not until the late Middle Ages that from the ranks of professional entertainers the actor emerged again in his own right. But his status was a precarious one. The Tudors did not approve of 'masterless men', that is those who had no settled occupation or were not apprenticed to a recognised trade or 'honest' profession. So the actor was classed as a rogue and vagabond, travelling the length of the land in search of an audience or patron prepared to pay for a show. Matters became worse in the early sixteenth century, and unless an actor could prove that he belonged to a nobleman's household (and was travelling with his permission) he was hounded by the authorities. With the building of the first permanent theatre building in the Elizabethan period the situation became more settled, but only for those lucky and talented enough to become members of established companies (technically household servants) such as the Admiral's Men or the Lord Chamberlain's Men. And although some celebrated performers such as Edward Alleyn, Richard Burbage and William Shakespeare did very well for themselves, the profession remained a lowly regarded one.

Matters did not improve when actresses first appeared on the scene – in the 1660s in England, earlier on the Continent. Immorality backstage and the practice of male members of the audience to visit the actresses' dressing-rooms after the show only tainted the image of the profession further. It is ironic that the introduction of women in Charles II's time had been on the moral grounds that the custom of having young boys and youths playing all the female roles 'might lead to abuse'! Certainly the ladies were enormously popular both on- and off-stage, but it was rare indeed for a Restoration actress not to be a 'kept woman'.

English Restoration theatre was greatly influenced by the contemporary French theatre, one of whose stars as actor and playwright was Molière. It is a measure of the outcast nature of the profession at this time that on Molière's death only an appeal by his widow to the King in person saved him from burial in unconsecrated ground. In England in the following century David Garrick, one of our most celebrated actors, who died in 1779, fared better. He was buried in Westminster Abbey, and the mourners stretched for miles. But for the less famous, their status remained low. It was not until the late nineteenth century that members of the acting profession began to be considered acceptable in polite society. The knighthood bestowed on Henry Irving in 1895 paved the way, and by the turn of the century several other eminent actor-managers had received the same accolade.

By the mid-twentieth century parents no longer threw up their hands in horror when their offspring expressed their intention of going on the stage. Conditions in the theatre were improving and actors were no longer at the mercy of unscrupulous managers who walked off with the box office receipts, leaving the cast stranded. Equity, the actors' trade union, set up as early as 1929, had become a watchdog regulating pay and conditions of employment. Drama became a widely accepted subject for study, university drama departments were established, and with a television set in almost every home successful actors became instant celebrities and lionised by the public. An air of glamour and a whiff of 'daringness' continue to cling to what is almost the oldest profession in the world.

the actor's
changing
status

acting styles

Acting styles have changed considerably since the time that Henry Irving dominated the stage. Irving believed that acting was for displaying the great passions; he concentrated on spectacular productions of Shakespeare and gave riveting performances of melodrama (see Chapter 11).

However, a new form of naturalistic drama began to appear around 1900. Plays were written in a more relaxed style and acting changed to reflect this elegance and naturalness. Art concealed art and the actor appeared not to be acting at all but simply behaving naturally. The epitome of such acting was Gerald Du Maurier, of whom Laurence Olivier remarked: 'Brilliant actor that he was, he had the most disastrous influence on my generation, because we really thought, looking at him, that it was easy; for the first ten years of our lives in the theatre, nobody could hear a word we said. We thought he was being really natural; of course, he was a genius of a technician giving that appearance, that's all.' Plays were often tailor-made to suit the easy style of leading actors such as Du Maurier, and because they were immensely popular and successful such actors had little urge or inclination to tackle the classics.

In the 1920s and early 1930s, during the aftermath of the First World War and the Depression, theatre audiences needed laughter and light entertainment, not heavy drama, and so the easy naturalistic style of acting continued. Then in the later 1930s came a renewed interest in Shakespeare and the classics, with the acting of such up-and-coming

Dame Edith Evans (1888–1976), one of the great actresses of the
English stage, seen here as Millamant in Congreve's *The Way of the
World* in 1927.

stars as Gielgud, Olivier, Richardson, Redgrave, Edith Evans,
Peggy Ashcroft, and Sybil Thorndike. Acting again became
powerful and physical, but this time without the Victorian
melodramatic bombast.

In modern times, particularly in the 1960s and 1970s,
acting has undergone a further radical change reflecting the
contemporary permissive society, the abolition of stage
censorship and the more outspoken nature of plays. Acting
has become more earthy, colloquial, and physical – the body is
now vitally important; vocal dexterity must be matched with
physical dexterity. Acting can have an edge of rawness about
it: the down-to-earth nature of contemporary drama involves

nudity, strong language and near-violent scenes. Removing one's clothes in public is today an actor's occupational hazard! Most actors today specialise in specific roles, but until a performer is established versatility is called for, combining the ability to cope with the classics (which demand intelligent and lyrical speaking) with a facility to grunt, sweat and swear in a modern play of rock-bottom realism.

what is great acting?

Crucial to this question is an understanding that basically there are two kinds of actor. First, there is the character actor who disguises his appearance and attempts a series of widely different roles, obliterating his own image in the process; and secondly there is the actor who is a 'self-impersonator', one who, no matter what part he plays, always presents *himself* – albeit in a slightly different guise, but one in which his own image is always predominant. Alec Guinness is an example of the first kind, Robert Morley of the second. This is not in any way to disparage either, for the profession itself recognises these two types of actor. Eric Porter, who crowned an already brilliant career in the theatre with his television portrayal of Soames in *The Forsyte Saga,* remarks: 'There are two kinds of actors. There are the actors who try to get completely away from themselves, put a great deal of make-up on – beards, moustaches, wigs, etc., – and virtually hide behind the *maquillage.* There are other actors who can only present themselves as if *they* were the part.' It was as true in the nineteenth century as it is today. Henry Irving said: 'There are only two ways of portraying a character on the stage. Either you can try to turn yourself into that person – which is impossible – or, and this is the way to act, you can take that person and turn him into yourself. That is how I do it!'

To every part an actor plays he brings something of his own personality. He cannot help but allow something of himself to shine through. The extent to which he allows his own persona to obtrude or be hidden depends on which of the two basic acting types he belongs to. In both cases, however, a good actor will use something of his own personality, find

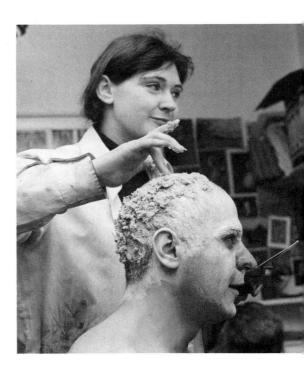

David Suchet being made up as Caliban in Shakespeare's *The Tempest*. In this production by Clifford Williams (RSC 1978), Caliban was presented as a black New World savage.

within himself a facet which fits the character he is playing. This is then brought into sharp focus, developed, then harnessed to the character being played and built up from there. This does not mean that the roles at which an actor is best are necessarily those closest to his own temperament, for the strongest responses are often those which in everyday life have to be suppressed and controlled. In acting, such held-down tendencies can be released and turned to advantage. Using such resources – the baser parts of one's own nature, so to speak – is not, as one might expect, potentially dangerous to the actor, but positively therapeutic. After playing a thoroughly evil and vicious character, it is not unusual for the actor to feel extremely composed and in a pleasant frame of mind, having, as it were, purged himself of such vicious tendencies. Dame Sybil Thorndike said that, after she had played one of the great classical viragos such as Medea, her friends and family always found her angelic!

So what is great acting and how can it be judged? It cannot be simply a measure of the extent to which an actor convinces us that he *is* the character he is impersonating, and

that his performance is the definitive interpretation – for there is no such thing. The playwright does not circumscribe his character in so exact a manner. Exactly who and what sort of man (or woman) is Hamlet, King Lear, Oedipus, Faustus, Hedda Gabler? The nature of the character changes subtly with every different performer. No two Hamlets are identical, still less King Lear. What is it, then, that bestows the accolade of 'great acting'?

The essence of acting is communication. If what the actor is doing on stage does not get across to his audience, he would be better employed elsewhere. The measure of an actor's skill is the vividness of his portrayal and how indelibly he imprints the thoughts and feelings of his role on the minds of his audience. And it should be remembered that a stage role is seldom static – the greatest acting parts are those in which the character experiences a variety and depth of emotion. In fact the classic definition of tragedy says that it is about a character who at the beginning of the play is happy and in an enviable position of eminence and prosperity only to fall into adversity due to some error of judgement and end his days wretchedly, dying as the curtain descends. Such a character has thus passed through the greatest possible change of circumstance. The actor's job is to convey the full magnitude and depth of feeling of such a catastrophe, so that the audience profoundly experiences the measure of the change. It is not enough that the tale be told – it must be *felt,* too.

Tragedy therefore provides the actor with the greatest possible scope for great acting; comedy or 'straight' plays contain fewer opportunities to run the gamut of emotion, for by definition a comedy ends happily, and even though disaster may threaten it never materialises. Furthermore, comedies usually contain more than one leading role; there is seldom a single, towering figure around whom the play revolves. Richard Burton says: 'The only kind of interesting parts to play are defeated men. That's why the great tragedies are so attractive to actors. One must always play a defeated man. The hero, the one who succeeds, is always faintly boring. Hamlet is a defeated man; Macbeth is a defeated man; Lear is a defeated man: they're all defeated men. Othello is; Iago is; Antony [in *Antony and Cleopatra*] fascinated me for that particular reason.' Such plays contain soliloquies and long speeches which provide the actor with the perfect launch pad: he is on his own – such scenes stand or fall by his sole effort. Inevitably Shakespeare springs to mind as providing some of the best vehicles for great acting – written (for a bonus) in his incomparable verse. Dame Sybil Thorndike felt that for great acting modern, purely realistic plays were not satisfactory vehicles; actors needed the great verse tragedies which required the use of the imagination in the performing of them. The verse 'kindles a fire', she comments, confirming that Shakespeare is indispensable to the 'great' actor.

In a quite different vein, but offering almost as rich an opportunity for great acting, are the plays of Chekhov – the second choice when actors speak of great acting roles – such as *The Seagull, Uncle Vanya, The Three Sisters,* and *The Cherry Orchard.* Chekhov is the master playwright of understatement, yet at the same time he provides the actor with enormous scope for conveying emotion and sensitivity. His plays are in prose – not prose of a 'literary' kind, but dialogue

The Three Sisters, Chekhov's masterly study of life's disillusions;
Trevor Nunn's studio production for the RSC 1979/80 with Suzanne
Bertish (Masha), Bridget Turner (Olga), Emily Richard (Irina).

written in a normal, simple, everyday style of speech.
Chekhov's characters are rich in pathos and offer marvellous
acting opportunities, especially to actresses, for he has created
some superb female roles.

It is often remarked that acting, on the rare occasions
when it might qualify for the epithet 'great', becomes instinc-
tive. The result is not the effect of studied art or clearly defined
technique, but of the actor being somehow 'taken over'. In
such moments, in actors' jargon, 'The god descends.' The
actor becomes inspired – he feels that something or someone
is taking him over and using his voice and body as an instru-
ment. He is acting, and yet at the same time apart from himself: a curious, dual feeling. An interesting anecdote is told of

Laurence Olivier, to whom 'the god descended' one night. The entire cast sensed that this performance was a great one, and when the curtain fell they were puzzled because Olivier immediately locked himself in his dressing-room and did not come out. Eventually, when he did emerge, he appeared low-spirited. When asked why, since everyone else thought he had given a tremendous performance, he himself wasn't elated, he replied that he was aware of this but was annoyed and perplexed because he could not analyse exactly how it had been achieved and it could not therefore be repeated to order!

The celebrated French actor Coquelin, who toured with Sarah Bernhardt and died in 1909, was right when he declared that the essential attributes of a good actor are a warm heart and a cool head. Great acting, however you define it – and it is re-defined in every age – is the result of these two attributes. The cool head contributes the technique which transmits the emotional responses of the heart, but never allows the passion to take over or run away with itself and the performance. If an actor loses control he loses his audience. On stage he may appear to be in a towering rage or sobbing uncontrollably, but his performance *is* under control; it has all been minutely planned.

Perhaps we shouldn't try to define great acting, but simply be enormously grateful when given the chance to witness it, and concentrate more on the effect such occasions have on both actors and audience. Whatever else it provides, great acting leaves marvellous memories. Irving summed it up: 'Acting may be evanescent, it may work in the media of a common nature, it may be mimetic like other arts . . . but it can live and can add to the sum of human knowledge in the ever varying study of man's nature . . . and can, like six out of the seven wonders of the world, exist as a great memory.'

4

HOW A PLAY BECOMES A PERFORMANCE

Getting a play on to a stage and ready to be seen by an audience is an excitingly creative but complex business. It starts like this:

Playwright   The playwright hands his play over to his agent (new hopefuls without an agent send their plays direct to theatre managements).

Agent   The agent finds a producer who is prepared to finance and present the play, negotiating with him the terms of the presentation and the playwright's fees/royalties. A fee known as a royalty is paid to the playwright for every performance given. In this way he shares the increased financial returns if the play is a success.

Producer
The producer engaged may be an impresario, an individual (e.g. Michael Codron or Corinne Graehame) or a company (e.g. Howard and Wyndham Ltd). The producer organises everything that has to be done to get a play in front of an audience and is responsible for all financial arrangements; he engages a director, signs up the stars, hires the rest of the players together with back-stage staff, finds a theatre, arranges publicity, and in consultation with the director commissions designers for scenery, costumes and lighting, etc.

Director
The director takes the actual rehearsals; he is responsible for how the play will look and sound on stage. He guides and directs the actors and discusses with the designers what he wants in the way of sets and costumes. He also plots with the technicians the required lighting and sound effects. He is the artistic interpreter of the playwright's work.

There still exists some confusion in the public mind over the use of the terms 'producer and director'. The producer's role is as described above; he does not direct rehearsals or shape the actors' performances artistically, or control or influence the final effect of the play in performance. These things are the province of the director. Their roles and responsibilities correspond exactly with those in the film industry. No confusion will arise if you remember the simple mnemonic, usually found in the programme of most professional productions, '. . . the production directed by . . .' The producer's job is to set up the production, a task which is largely administrative and financial. The artistic direction of the play is in the hands of the director alone.

angels

Money has to be found to pay all the bills incurred during the set-up and before the play gets into a theatre and starts its run. Once the play has opened, of course, the sums spent can hopefully be recovered from the box office receipts, but before this happens the cost of scenery and costumes, the salaries of actors and stage staff during the rehearsal period, the fees of the director and designers, as well as administrative costs, all have to be met. This is where the theatrical term 'angel' comes in. Angels are financial backers who advance hard cash to the producer, investing in a production in the hope that the show will be a smash hit and give them a good return on their money. Angels have to be gamblers, too, for there is no known recipe for a theatrical success. If the play closes after the opening performances, all the money invested is lost.

special company staff

If the production is a small-scale one mounted by an impresario and not by a production company, he and his assistants will personally cope with its setting up. If, however, the production is a large-scale one being produced by a company, the company will have its own staff which will include:

The *general business manager* is responsible for all contracts and financial arrangements. He prepares budgets, detailing all likely production expenses, the estimated box office income and the likelihood of profitable returns.

The *production manager* will be an experienced person of the theatre capable of dealing with all technical aspects of mounting a show, including lighting, sound and wardrobe.

The *publicity and press representative* will create and maintain interest in the company's current and forthcoming productions.

During the set-up period and for each specific production there will be a creative team working with the play's director.

company manager
(the producer's business representative)

working with the

director

who will have the following creative team

actors
(the cast)

designer(s)
there may be two,
one each for

scenery   **costumes**

lighting designer
and if necessary
sound specialist

stage manager
and assistants

When this creative team has done its job, when all the details of setting, scenery, props, costumes, sound and lighting have been settled, the sets built, the costumes made, and the play fully rehearsed and awaiting an audience, the production is ready to go into a theatre.

In the theatre a further team is involved – the people who will operate and maintain the production throughout its run. Because most commercial theatres are rented out to the company presenting a play (the company does not own the theatre or 'live' there permanently) two sets of people are often involved: the permanent (resident) back-stage staff of the theatre hired, and the company back-stage crew of the play being presented.

permanent back-stage staff in major theatres

Here, the divisions of responsibility back-stage are as follows.

The *master carpenter* is the senior member of the back-stage staff. Sometimes called the resident stage manager or stage director, he is in charge of the fabric and mechanical equipment of the stage, and is responsible for supervising the stage setting and the handling of all scenery.

He may be assisted by a couple of day-men, experienced stage-hands who, apart from assisting the master carpenter in maintenance work, supervise stage staff at performances of 'heavy' (big and complicated) productions.

permanent back-stage staff

The *chief electrician* superintends the lighting of a production and is in charge of all stage lighting equipment. He is also responsible for the maintenance of all electrical and mechanical equipment in the theatre.

The *property master* creates and looks after 'props' and maintains stage furniture and the objects used in dressing the set. All articles used during a performance are his responsibility.

The *wardrobe mistress*, with her assistants, helps the costume designer to provide or make the costumes and afterwards to repair and clean them. She is knowledgeable on period costume and capable of cutting out and making up complete costumes herself. She arranges dressers for the artistes and is often responsible additionally for the cleaners in the theatre — in which case she would be known as the house-keeper.

All major large theatres, such as the Palladium and Drury Lane, have a permanent staff of such key figures, together with a stage-door keeper and fireman. When each new show starts its run, these permanent staff are augmented by the company crew of that show who have been specially engaged for its run. Thus in the setting up of a play, when the company moves into a large theatre it would have the above-mentioned permanent or resident staff of that theatre to advise and assist it, but the day-to-day running of the actual performances would be the responsibility of the company's own crew. Some members of this back-stage crew would have already been working with the cast during rehearsals in the setting-up period.

company back-stage crew

A typical crew to operate a simple small-scale production in the theatre would comprise the following:

**company
back-stage
crew**

The *stage manager* is in charge of the stage and has over-all responsibility for the running of the play. In small productions he or she might also be the company manager.

The *deputy stage manager (DSM)* usually operates and supervises each nightly performance.

Assistant stage managers (ASMs) help shift scenery and furniture, make available 'props' and generally assist in the presentation of a show.

The *lighting operator* controls and operates the many lighting effects required on-stage, as well as dimming and raising the auditorium lights.

The *sound operator* controls the recorded sound effects used during the play, such as telephones, doorbells, car noises, wind and rain sounds, etc., as well as playing recorded music relayed to the auditorium before and after the performance, and during intervals

The *wardrobe supervisor* ensures that costumes are clean and pressed for every performance, and is ready to carry out any immediate repairs.

Staff and conditions vary from theatre to theatre and are directly related to the size of the theatre and the nature of the production being staged. Musical shows, for instance, require a large extra team in the set-up period – the musical director, musicians, rehearsal pianist, choreographer and so on, as well as extra back-stage staff in the theatre during the run to cope with such a 'heavy' production. The number of permanent back-stage staff employed by a small provincial repertory theatre will probably be only half a dozen, but by contrast large organisations like the National Theatre and the Royal Shakespeare Company employ very many times this number, being equipped with their own workshops and employing specialists such as metalworkers, an armourer and a wig mistress.

Thus the set-up and the run have two distinct but overlapping organisations. The set-up administration ceases with the opening-night performance, after which the responsibility for the run is entirely in the hands of the cast, the company's stage manager and his/her back-stage crew.

stage management

Efficient stage management is an art – a vital part of a theatre performance of which an audience is usually totally unaware. This is as it should be – it gives enormous satisfaction to those who have chosen stage management as a career in theatre to pilot the play silently and satisfactorily to its final curtain. And because every performance is a live one, there is always the risk that something might go wrong. For instance a 'prop' may suddenly go missing or break and a substitute must be instantly found; or an actor has dropped or left something on-stage which must be recovered before the next scene.

If you have ever wondered how, during the course of a very brief blackout, an entire scene change can be so quickly accomplished, the stage-hands can tell you. It is done by one of several methods:

1 The stage itself revolves, bringing into view a completely new scene (already set) as the old one disappears.

2 The new setting is 'trucked on' – i.e. already set up on a movable platform (a boat-truck) waiting in the wings. The 'old' setting is also on a boat-truck, which slides off-stage as the new one trucks on.

3 The scenery is 'flown' (in sections). Large pieces of scenery are lashed together, then fixed to a batten lifted bodily via a wire-roped counterweight pulley system into the roof of the stage (the flies) where it hangs out of sight. The new scenery (hung by the same system but on different 'lines') is lowered ('let in'). These operations are done by 'fly-men'.

4 The scenery 'sinks'. This happens only in major theatres where hydraulic lifts have been installed in sections ('bridges') across the entire stage area. As the scenery sinks below the stage, new scenery rises to take its place.

Getting rid of scenery (or even a piece of stage furniture) is known as 'striking it'; putting up scenery is 'setting it'.

A daily task of stage-hands (but again only in the larger traditional theatres) is 'dropping the iron', which is not as clumsy as it sounds – it is merely the lowering and raising of the safety curtain (usually made of iron sheets) which is required by fire regulations to be done at every performance. This is to reassure the audience that, in the event of a fire on-stage, they will be safe.

The introduction of sophisticated sound equipment and the widespread use of the magnetic tape recorder have reduced the number of ASMs required to run a show. Not so very long ago many of the standard back-stage sound effects were achieved manually – the turning of the wind and rain machines, the closing of a contraption to simulate a slamming door, the sound of a crash (by pouring broken glass from one box into another); but nowadays, apart from 'ringing' tele-phone bells, only one regularly hand-operated sound effect seems to have survived – the thunder sheet. This is a large sheet of metal hung up back-stage: it has two handles on its bottom edge which are grasped and yanked back and forth to produce from the waving sheet a very convincing sound like thunder. In the march of time, other traditional theatrical back-stage jobs have gone or are gradually disappearing. Call-boys no longer race up and down back-stage corridors knocking on dressing-room doors warning actors of their impending entrance cues – calling is now more effortlessly achieved by means of loudspeakers in each dressing-room (and elsewhere back-stage), fed from the control room and operated by the stage management team. The same loud-speakers, by the way, are connected to microphones on-stage so that the progress of the play is simultaneously, quietly, 'broadcast' to everyone back-stage.

Even the unthinkable has happened in some theatres – the prompt has gone. Prompting was usually undertaken by stage management personnel who also cued in sound and lighting effects; it was known as 'being on the book'. In most theatres such cues are now operated from control rooms at the back of the auditorium (which give a better and clearer view of the stage) and not from the side of the stage as previously. Companies cannot therefore afford the luxury of employing an ASM on-stage in the wings throughout an entire perform-ance merely to prompt, so in many theatres the actors are on their own!

But however important the back-stage crews are in maintaining a play in fine shape throughout its run in the theatre, remember that it is the director who originally visualised it that way and has arranged it.

the director's relationship with the designers

Like a ship's helmsman, the director steers the play and ensures that the contributions of the cast and of the designers of sets, costumes and lighting all contribute towards *his* interpretation. The designers are there not to impose their own ideas on a production but to carry out those of the director. At their first meetings the director will have indicated the approach he is adopting, and it is the designers' task to interpret his wishes to the best of their abilities. For instance, in a production of *Hamlet* the director might inform the scenic designer that he does not want the stage sets to be replicas of parts of Kronberg Castle, Elsinore, Denmark (where according to the play's text the action takes place) but that he wants an abstract setting, a series of different levels, ramps and steps not anchored in time and space, so as to give the play universality and depth and the better to re-create the sweeping action of the play without pausing for scene changes. He might advise the costume designer that he does not want the play dressed in the traditional Elizabethan period costumes, but, say, in a non-contemporary style belonging to no one specific period and with colours restricted to muted tones. To the lighting designer he will indicate which scenes must be brilliantly lit and which require only dim lighting.

The style and mood of a play should be reflected in its settings and costumes, a point clearly made in the recent Royal Shakespeare Company's enormously successful production of *Nicholas Nickleby*, adapted from the Dickens novel. The basic setting deserved the highest praise in that it did not look designed – though clearly it must have been. It looked as though it had always been there and had just accumulated. The open stage, apart from a small central clear space, was cluttered both at floor level and above with impedimenta of every description: baggage, trunks, furniture, objects, clothes, ornaments, etc., in a glorious jumble of useful and useless decorative lumber. High above stage level,

This photograph captures the bustle and vigour of Trevor Nunn's imaginative production of *Nicholas Nickleby* at the RSC. The 'coach' was created by piled-up baggage.

walkways and suggestions of chimneys and rooftops contributed to an overwhelming sense of Victorian life – busy,
populated, cramped, huddled, tangled, and overflowing with
bric-à-brac. Lighting effects contributed dark gloomy patches
offset by shafts of light. Immediately one was plunged into
the teeming life of Victorian times and the slightly down-at-
heel world in which Dickens' tale mostly takes place. It was a
masterly conception on the part of the designer and director,
and prepared the audience instantly for what was to follow.

Costumes are an obvious point of interest, but a clever
designer can manipulate an audience's feelings in both bold
and subtle ways. No one who saw it will ever forget the
breathtaking impact of the Ascot scene in the original production of *My Fair Lady*. Cecil Beaton had dressed the entire
company in black and white to create an effect of devastating
elegance. On a less obvious level, a woman dressed in twin set
and pearls or a man wearing a tie and a dark three-piece suit
on a hot summer's day will immediately be informative to an
audience. Whether the costumes are to give a fashion-plate
effect or imply an everyday reality must also be decided by
director and designer. An elegant, artificial comedy such as
Oscar Wilde's *The Importance of Being Earnest* should never
have its bloom sullied by a hint of the workaday world, and its
costumes must therefore be unusually elegant. In contrast, a
play such as *The Lower Depths* (1902) by the Russian playwright Gorky will fail unless its costumes look as though they
have been lived, eaten and slept in for years.

Most costume designers will deliberately limit their
colour range when designing a production, using only one
part of the colour spectrum, and in so doing will achieve a
pleasing over-all homogeneous effect. Colours are often
described as warm or cold and designers will use them
accordingly. An elderly, frigid spinster would not be appro-
priately costumed in warm pink or peach tones; a 'scarlet
woman', however, is aptly so named and dressed. The
costume designer, if he or she is not also responsible for the
sets, must work closely with the set designer. It is pointless
attempting to create a stunning entrance for an actress dressed in a particular primary colour if the background setting is
in the same colour.

the director's relationship with the designers

Qualities of warmth and coldness are also inherent in certain lighting effects (over and above those reflecting seasonal changes and the time of day). Though probably quite unaware of it, an audience is often influenced by the lighting designer's ability to create a feeling of a certain kind with light alone. In intimate love scenes, for instance, the general over-all lighting on-stage will be lowered slightly and the couple bathed in a warmish light to reflect their absorption in each other and the glowing intensity of their feelings. Most audiences probably do not realise that coloured lighting plays an important part; white light alone is seldom used as it gives too cold an effect. Stage lights operate through coloured filters, the colours themselves carefully chosen so that every scene in the play is subtly and effectively lit. The effect of a particular costume or scene in a play can be enhanced or ruined by the lighting designer's work. An extravagant ball dress in a particular colour will be shown to its best advantage if lit with the same hue, but dulled and diminished in tone if lit by a complementary colour. Since it is seldom possible for an actress to be covered on stage wherever she moves by lamps of a particular hue, this can cause problems.

Basically the lighting designer has four ways of achieving his effects; by varying the intensity, colour, and direction of the light and by controlling the size of area illuminated. Directional lighting of itself can conjure up remarkable atmospheric effects, such as the dark obscurity of a prison cell lit only by thin shafts of light falling through a barred window high up in a wall.

All the designers, therefore, must work together to reinforce and convey the image of the play which the director has decided upon, each complementing the others' work. Next time you see a play, ask yourself to what extent these elements of costume, set design and lighting contributed to the success of the production — or, if unsuccessful, what they failed to contribute.

the theatre manager

Apart from the actors and the director, the general public is unlikely to know by name, or have much opportunity of contact with, the producers and set, costume and lighting designers involved in the preparation of a play for the theatre. The one person, however, they are most likely to meet (and of whose existence they should certainly know) is the theatre manager. In very large city theatres he may be represented by his front-of-house manager, but in smaller theatres the manager himself may well be found in the theatre foyer, especially at the end of an evening performance, assessing its reception and welcoming the chance of a few words with his patrons.

Theatre managers are the direct link between the public and the producer, and a recognised channel of communication between them. In many small theatres it is the theatre manager himself who actually books in all productions to his theatre, so he clearly has a vested interest in their receptions. All theatre managers are anxious to fill their theatres, so no audience member should hesitate to approach them with his or her views on the kind of show they would like to see. Of course, the theatre manager himself has no part in the production and preparation of the play he presents in his theatre; like any other entrepreneur he merely books a show into his 'shop' for consumption by the public, though naturally he will satisfy himself beforehand of the company's credentials and standards.

From this brief summary of the setting up of a play, it will be abundantly clear that far from the actors being responsible for everything, and far from making it all up as they go along, an enormous amount of time and a very large number of people are involved in preparing even the most simple and straightforward of plays for a run in a theatre. When criticising a play after a performance, therefore, one needs to be able to sort out and assess the contribution of everyone involved; to distinguish between the playwright's intentions as he wrote the play and the director's realisation and interpretation of it; the actors' inherent talents and the director's insistence on a particular style of acting; and the assistance given by the designers of sets, costumes and lighting. Because of the close teamwork that is essential in the theatre, separating out these components is often no easy matter even for the experts. We often speak of 'the star of the show' – but is there indeed any such individual?

5

THE PRIMITIVE ORIGINS OF THEATRE

What we see in today's theatres – the kind of play, the nature of the production, the style of acting, even the shape of the theatre building – bears little resemblance to drama as initially practised. Today's theatre is the result of an almost continuous period of development over several thousand years. How did it all begin? It is easy enough to appreciate that the drama of the fifteenth century should differ from that of the twentieth, but when and how and why and where did dramatic performances emerge in the first place?

No one really knows the answers to these questions; the origins of drama are complex and remote, involving a study not only of the earliest civilisations but of man himself. However, two or three suggestions have been put forward, of which the first, and by far the most important, concerns man's own behaviour. Man possesses an in-built mimetic instinct – that is to say, he has a habit of imitating or mimicking things and people. Allied with this, two other factors are thought to be important in considering the origins of drama. They are ancient folk ceremonies and religious ceremony; common to both is the concept of ritual.

Ritual is an action or procedure followed solemnly, conducted usually with splendour, and always with fervour. It gives both shape and meaning to an event, binds people together, asserts their membership of a community, giving them a sense of belonging, reinforces their faiths and beliefs, and confers a sense of well-being. From the very earliest times man knew the benefits of ritual, especially in the practice of religion.

Ritual was also connected with ancient folk ceremonies, particularly those of hunting and agriculture; primitive man created and worshipped gods of the earth and sky to assist him in hunting and to help his crops grow and his cattle breed. In creating such ritual, man's mimetic instincts were given full play, and music, even if it were only the beating of a drum, was also employed together with dance. (Dance, in many early communities, was regarded in the same sense as prayer.) These activities arose because of primitive man's desire to call upon and influence or thank the life-giving forces, felt by him to be spirits or gods; the most important of these spirits was the god of fertility.

Examples of folk ritual, vestiges of which are still practised today, are rural May Day ceremonies performed at the onset of spring. Maypoles were erected and garlanded, and the revellers decked in flowers and greenery. Music was provided and dances were performed around the maypole. All this was done to encourage the fresh green shoots of spring — in which it was thought the spirit of the god resided — to grow big and strong. The burgeoning spirit of fertility was being worshipped and encouraged.

Another direct descendant of early folk ritual, and more obviously cast in dramatic form, is mummers' plays. These plays are clearly connected with the spirit of fertilisation or regeneration, for the central feature is invariably a fight in which one of the contestants is killed and then brought back to life again. Such a character may be called St George or Hector or Bold Slasher; the dialogue is of the simplest, the action of the crudest, and the play extremely short, but such plays always include a 'doctor' figure who, with charming, sometimes alarming nonsense and hocus-pocus, brings back to life the slain 'hero'. Such action betokens man's concern with maintaining the cyclic saga of birth, growth, decay and rebirth observable in the seasons, when spring grows to summer, declines into autumn and seems to die in winter. 'Magic' ensures the continuation of the cycle, the rebirth of spring. Thus in the mummers' plays the cycle of life was being enacted, and by repeated performance was sustaining and encouraging the magic to continue. Morris dancing, sword dances, May Day celebrations and mummers' plays are all remnants of ritual folk activity stretching back into the mists of time. They represent one of the earliest links in the chain of the story from ritual to drama. A clearer link, however, is to be found in religious ceremony.

When in the course of time, religious creeds developed and a specific one became adopted by a tribe or race as the 'state' religion, religious ceremony advanced considerably. Greater ceremony and a constant repetition of devotions expanded the ritual. Into this ritual was gradually introduced the representation of stories of the gods, incorporating impersonation, dialogue and costume. Such ingredients are the essence of drama and ritual drama grew and flourished.

The emergence of a 'play' as such, and the creation of a special theatre space in which to perform it, took time. The details are uncertain. The earliest ritual performances that developed into a form we recognise as 'drama' occurred in Ancient Greece (see Chapter 6). There are hints that earlier forms existed in Ancient Egypt, India and the Far East, but not enough evidence has survived to establish this in fact. With Ancient Greece we are on surer ground: not only have many of the plays themselves come down to us, but we can still visit the architectural sites or theatres where the plays were once performed, and pictorial evidence is further available from paintings on pottery. We even have some notes written by the earliest known drama critic, Aristotle, which tell us a great deal about the theory of Greek theatre practice. By the fifth century BC, in the period known as the Golden Age of Greece, individual, sophisticated pieces of religious and folk ritual were being performed – Aristotle later called them 'imitations of actions'. The 'play' had been conceived – a form of dramatised poetry with music and dance in honour of the gods.

During the following centuries, when pagan religions

had given way to Christianity in Europe, religious drama continued to be encouraged by the now established Catholic Church, and from about the tenth century AD was widely performed. Eventually, after centuries of religious plays (and the still continuing folk drama), drama finally disengaged itself from its religious mould, to become a secular activity standing on its own two feet and practised for itself alone.

The importance of ritual in the story of drama lies not only in the significance of the event being celebrated, but in the creation and communication of an emotional response – the by-product of ritual. For the exciting experience conjured up by the service or ceremony, the solemnity of the occasion and the ordered procedure of the rites, evokes an emotional response in those taking part which creates a bond between them. This response affects equally those who perform the rites (initially the witch doctors, priests, prophets, wise men, elders or leaders) and those who merely witness or assist (the community). The experience is heightened by music, dancing and singing and the costumes of the participants. This emotional response is a further link between ritual and the emergence of drama, for the feeling generated is similar. Onstage in the modern theatre an atmosphere is created which communicates itself to the audience. If a performance is successful, then in theatrical parlance 'it has worked'. When it works, the audience is profoundly moved – to sympathy, approval, tears, laughter, even anger. If a performance 'leaves you cold', then it has not worked.

Of course, the nature of the experience felt by primitive man thousands of years ago at some ancient rite, and that felt by an audience in a modern theatre, are rather different. In the first a direct assault is made on the senses, particularly those of sight and sound. Today there is the additional element of an appeal to the intellect through the play's text (a late addition in the development of drama), which expounds a theory or promotes a philosophy and therefore requires consideration. But a great deal of theatre today is still of an elemental kind, making an assault primarily on the eyes and ears with little involvement of the intellect. One of the vitally important responses still prevailing in theatre today depends on what the actor does, not necessarily on what he says.

6

ANCIENT GREECE AND ROME

Ancient Greek drama

Performances of drama in ancient Greece were vivid affairs; they were religious and civic occasions to which the entire community flocked. Plays were only performed on special occasions at great festivals lasting from dawn to dusk, and for several days at a time: the main festivals were held in January–February and March–April. The celebrations took place in specially created open-air theatres that held thousands of spectators. All the performances were dedicated to the god Dionysus, a nature god of fertility, also known particularly, though not exclusively, as the wine god, representing the spirit of bacchic revelry or irrationality. There are associations here with the grape harvest, when in earlier times choral odes were composed and sung in honour of the god – and no doubt much sampling of the product was indulged in. Although all Greek cities were thought to possess their own theatres, Athens was pre-eminent and all the plays that have come down to us are Athenian, dating from the fifth and fourth centuries BC. All the parts were played by men, for no women were allowed on the Greek stage.

Greek plays are stylised and not naturalistic dramas, as is evident from their structure and the fact that the 'action' is broken up by the dancing and chanting of a chorus. A Greek play consists of a series of episodes, which relate the plot of the play, alternating with choral odes by a chorus ranging in number from fifteen to fifty, which comment on it. The plays were rhetorically delivered, there was little stage action or business, and all the actors wore large masks and special costumes. The stylised delivery was in keeping with the heightened poetic language in which the plays were written. Nothing could be more different from a modern play. Moreover, almost without exception the plots were extremely well known to the audience, being taken from familiar stories of the exploits of their gods and goddesses and legendary heroes.

Although hundreds of plays must have been written during Greece's Golden Age, only a small fraction have survived, all mainly written by the prizewinning playwrights Aeschylus, Sophocles and Euripides (the religious festivals at which the plays were performed offered prizes for the best plays in honour of the god). The names of other victors are recorded, but their plays have not survived.

In the century following the Golden Age lived Aristotle, theatregoer, critic, teacher and philosopher. He attempted to analyse Greek drama and left us (albeit in imperfect form) his deliberations on the subject, entitled *The Poetics.* Aristotle codified the plays and defined tragedy. Briefly, he said that it is the 'imitation of an action' (i.e. it is something done, not simply recited or narrated); that it is serious and significant; that it is written in a heightened form of language; with a plot which has a beginning, middle and an end, containing incidents arousing pity and fear; and that it provides an outlet for such emotions (catharsis). The play's intention is to show how the central character (protagonist), an eminent man and a good one, who enjoys high status, suffers an unexpected change of fortune, falling from happiness into adversity through some catastrophe as a result of a grave mistake, or a fatal flaw in his otherwise admirable character.

Ancient Greek drama

Therefore tragedy necessarily dealt with people in high places and always ended unhappily. It was exemplary drama. A good example is Sophocles' *Oedipus.*

In contrast, comedy, Aristotle continued, dealt with the lower classes, exhibiting the 'worst kind of men' who indulged in ridiculous or mistaken behaviour (the common errors of mankind), but with no lasting harm or pain to others – of the kind, rather, which induced laughter. He left only snippets of text devoted to comedy, spending most of his book discussing tragedy as the more superior form of drama. Although he himself could never have met Aeschylus, Sophocles or Euripides, or seen the original productions of their prizewinning plays, he acknowledged their superiority and cited examples of their work.

Greek drama is perhaps one of the most difficult forms of drama to understand, yet undeniably in production it has immense theatrical potential. Greek tragedy is rightly regarded as one of the supreme forms of drama, but a full understanding presupposes considerable knowledge of the life and times of Ancient Greece, and above all of the Greeks' religious views and attitudes to their gods. The Greek gods play a central role in the plays (usually unseen, though not always so) yet the gods can in no way be equated with a Christian God. The Greeks regarded their lives as controlled by their gods: what happened in life was the direct result of pleasing or displeasing one of their many deities. Such gods had specific attributes, and proper worship and attention needed to be given them. To ignore or defy one of the deities inevitably had serious consequences. Above all, disaster always ensued if you behaved not as a mortal, but with pride and arrogance (*hubris*), putting yourself above others and presuming a divine superiority. The plays themselves are not difficult to follow; the stories they tell are simple enough, but their significance and interpretation are less obvious. For example, let's take a look at Euripides' play *Hippolytus.*

Opposite: An incident from the RSC's marathon *The Greeks* (Jan. 1980) based on plays by Aeschylus, Sophocles and Euripides recounting the legendary Trojan War and its aftermath.

Ancient Greek drama

The plot is quickly told. It deals with Theseus, his young second wife Phaedra, and Hippolytus, Theseus' son by his first wife. When the play opens, Theseus is away from home and his wife Phaedra has fallen in love with her stepson. Hippolytus, however, will have nothing to do with her and rather brutally scorns her. In the grip of an immense passion, Phaedra languishes and pines away, and to end her dilemma commits suicide, leaving a note implicating Hippolytus. Theseus returns, learns of his wife's suicide, reads the note and instantly believes that Hippolytus has raped Phaedra and that she has killed herself to avoid dishonour. Theseus calls down a curse on his son which is almost immediately fulfilled; Hippolytus is mortally wounded. The truth is then revealed, but Theseus is too late to save his son. Alone, he mourns the loss of both his wife and son.

The significance of the play far surpasses its simple telling. The play is written with the gods omnipresent. It deals with the rival forces of passion and chastity, embodied in the goddesses Aphrodite and Artemis. Not only do these powerful goddesses appear in the play as themselves, but statues of both stand on either side of the stage throughout the play, mute testimony (until they come alive) of the opposing forces acting on the leading characters. These goddesses are shown as vindictive powers venting destruction on those who do not acknowledge or worship them. Hippolytus dedicates himself only to Artemis, the virgin huntress, patroness of chastity; he spends all his time hunting, ignoring Aphrodite, goddess of sexual love and passion. It is explained in the play that Aphrodite has caused Phaedra to fall in love with Hippolytus in order to destroy him, because he has ignored Aphrodite and worshipped only Artemis. In the eyes of the Ancient Greeks, the catastrophe is due entirely to the invincible commands of rival goddesses, but to us it is all too understandable in human terms. From a modern point of view, the tragedy might be supposed to be that of Phaedra, but Euripides called the play *Hippolytus* to draw attention to *his* nature and behaviour.

An interpretation of the play would suggest that to deny the natural impulses within us, and to which all humanity is subject, is to court disaster. In terms of this play, one should neither be rigid enough to exclude passion, nor susceptible enough to be consumed by it. The play advocates the 'golden mean' – to which idea the Greeks returned time and again: indulge in nothing to excess. It cautions against pride and hastiness, but above all against succumbing to an absolute consuming passion.

Greek dramatists used familiar legends and tales to reflect contemporary individual or community problems. Their plays dealt objectively with human behaviour – though interpreted as influenced by the gods – and with the problems of leadership and government. In tragedy these issues were seriously explored, but in comedy they were made fun of. Greek comedy has been described as obscene, and certainly to some people the ubiquitous use of huge replicas of the male sexual organ (*phalloi* – worn as part of the costume for comedy) might be considered objectionable. Aristophanes and Menander were the two major comic playwrights. Greek comedy was irreverent, bawdy, Rabelaisian, fantastic and riotously funny; it did not hesitate to lampoon contemporary events, people and practices. It, too, used a chorus which danced and chanted, and was often drawn from the realms of fantasy with choruses representing wasps, frogs or birds – the names by which some of Aristophanes' comedies are known.

Greek theatres

The very earliest Greek theatres were simply levelled spaces in the open air, roughly circular, at the foot of some con-venient hillside which provided the 'grandstand' from which the onlookers watched. By the fourth century BC this basic arrangement was surfaced in stone, and had the addition, opposite the tiered seating, of a narrow raised stage backed by a structure of wood or stone, called the *skene* building, re-sembling the façade of a palace. The actors performing the episodes did so on this separate stage, from which steps led on to a large flat circular stone floor at ground level, called the *orchestra*. It is here that the chorus danced and chanted. (The modern term 'orchestra stalls' in theatres meaning seats nearest the stage, is derived from this – it has nothing to do with a band!)

**Greek
theatres**

One of the most important aspects of Greek theatre was the contribution of the chorus as they danced and chanted their choral odes, weaving patterns of movement on the orchestra floor, but remaining silent and attentive during the acted episodes. Blessed with an ideal climate for open-air theatre, and with performances regarded as religious occasions and wealthily sponsored, the Greeks would have been able to enjoy impressive productions on a grand scale.

Ancient Rome

As the glories of Ancient Greece faded the Roman world began to emerge. By the end of the first century AD the Romans had conquered most of Europe and the Mediterranean world, and adopted or adapted much of Greek art. Theatre continued to flourish but in a somewhat debased form. Tragedy failed to achieve the heights gained by Greece, but comedy blossomed and developed. Roman drama has been described as spectacular, excessive and sensual. On the one hand enormous amphitheatres like the Colosseum and the Circus Maximus in Rome were filled with quasi-dramatic spectacles, and on the other hand plays were presented in more modest theatre buildings (still open-air), based on the Greek model but much reduced in size; the Romans cut the orchestra floor in half – from a circle to a semi-circle. Where Greek tragedy offered quality, the Romans offered quantity. We hear in some instances of huge parades of horses, camels and mules filing across the stage in Roman versions of Greek tragedies. Drama had to compete with extremely popular circus-type entertainments and mime shows, and rather lost out to them.

Greek tragedy was avidly though lamely copied, and of the Roman tragic playwrights only Seneca is noteworthy. His work may be considered sensational – in the pejorative sense! He wrote some ten tragedies, all written in a form similar to the Greek pattern, maintaining the same structure of alternating episodes and choric odes and using for his plots the ancient myths and legends. His style of writing has given rise to the term 'Senecan', indicating drama that is violent,

disparing
depreciating

bloodthirsty and rhetorical. His plays are mainly horror stories of revenge, containing atrocities and supernatural agents; the dialogue is liberally sprinkled with pithy maxims. The plays closely resemble Greek tragic drama in external and formal characteristics, but are devoid of the Greek inner informing spirit. His tragedies are termed 'closet dramas', for there is no evidence that they were ever performed publicly; it is thought they were recited at private gatherings.

A typical Senecan tragedy is his *Thyestes,* based on the Greek story of the hatred of two brothers. One of them, whose wife has been raped by his brother, revenges himself by appearing to offer friendship and forgiveness, and invites his brother to a solemn feast. The chief dish at the feast, however, turns out to be his brother's children chopped up and roasted. The truth is revealed only after the brother has gorged himself on his own children's flesh. Seneca influenced many later playwrights with his particular style, especially in the creation of a very popular Elizabethan genre known as revenge tragedy.

Roman comedy is far more important and interesting; it dispensed with the chorus and choral odes (which Menander had initiated in Greek new comedy), resulting in comedy of a more narrative and naturalistic structure. Plautus and Terence, the chief Roman comic dramatists, portrayed the vicissitudes of the common man and dealt mainly with stock situations and characters: the trials and tribulations of servants and masters, the amorous intrigues of the young, mistaken identity and misunderstandings. Using a basic comic formula, the plays began unhappily with some upset or other, but drew to a happy conclusion. Plautus and Terence were the first playwrights to discover and successfully exploit a comic formula. The wily and resourceful servant, the lecherous old master, the young amorous 'blade' and the long-lost child are the sort of characters they handled effectively. Such comedy is bright, witty, pleasant, fast-moving, and occasionally bawdy.

With the decline of the Roman world in the fifth century AD drama faded too. The Barbarians were not interested in it, and during the centuries of the so-called Dark Ages regular professional and public theatre ceased and the buildings crumbled into disuse. The many out-of-work actors, mime and pantomime artists took to the road, offering entertainment wherever they could, giving solo recitals and performances of physical 'feats of activity'. The mime was unmasked acting – a revolutionary form of drama in classical times when no self-respecting actor would dream of appearing without his mask. Mime artists were low-class performers and depended for their effects on exaggerated physical gesture, especially of facial expression. Performances were largely improvised, sub-literary, and usually quite short. Although such performances relied almost exclusively on physical action and sound effects, it was not unusual for mimes to incorporate dialogue.

During the last years of the Roman Empire and with the growing spread of Christianity, some telling comments of Roman theatre remain to illumine it for us. In the late fourth century AD John Chrysostom, one of the greatest of early Christian theologians, remarked that the theatre was '. . . the seat of pestilence, the gymnasium of incontinence and a school of luxury [lechery]. Satan being the author and architect of it.' He went on to say that gross comedies, indecent ballets and ribald pantomime were the rule; marriage was constantly mocked, even the eucharist was burlesqued, and the *pièce de résistance* was often the frolic of nude courtesans in specially constructed swimming pools; '. . . their songs were unashamedly coarse, with such a theme as how a woman loved a man, and not obtaining him, hanged herself.' Even making allowances for his somewhat biased viewpoint (the early Christians would not admit actors as converts unless they gave up their profession), the picture is clear enough.

7

MEDIEVAL DRAMA

the religious background

With the establishment of Christianity came an age of faith throughout medieval Europe, in which the way of life was dominated by the church. The practice of drama which had survived the classical world only in fragments – wandering entertainers and rural folk customs – was gradually brought into focus again when the Christian church adopted ritual drama as it increased its own religious rites and ceremonies. The church used ritual drama to educate the unlearned and to strengthen the faith of the newly converted. It was first employed in the liturgy (church services), and there is evidence that by the tenth century AD its use was widespread throughout Europe. Liturgical drama, as it is called, although 'performed' was chanted not spoken, was always in Latin and not in the vernacular, and formed an integral part of the church service. It was therefore a form of worship and in no sense intended as entertainment; nevertheless such activities were irrefutably theatrical, involving impersonation (with symbolic costumes and 'props'), dialogue and action.

The best-known of the early liturgical dramas is the
Quem Quaeritis, (Latin, meaning 'Whom seek ye?') and
belongs to the service of Matins on Easter morning. The dialogue is taken from the gospel account of the Easter story of
the risen Christ, condensed into a few lines of question and
answer and performed ritualistically.

Angel:　　　　　　　　*Quem quaeritis in sepulchro,*
　　　　　　　　　　　　O Christicolae?
　　　　　　　　　　　　(Whom seek ye in the tomb, O followers
　　　　　　　　　　　　of Christ?)

The Three Marys:　　*Ihesum Nazarenum crucifixum*
　　　　　　　　　　　　O celicola.
　　　　　　　　　　　　(Jesus of Nazareth who was crucified,
　　　　　　　　　　　　O Heavenly One.)

Angel:　　　　　　　　*Non est hic; surrexit, sicut praedixerat:*
　　　　　　　　　　　　Ite, nuntiate quia surrexit a mortuis.
　　　　　　　　　　　　(He is not here, He has risen as He said;
　　　　　　　　　　　　Go announce that He has risen from the
　　　　　　　　　　　　dead.)

The directions for the service clearly state: 'These things are
done indeed, in representation of the angel sitting within the
tomb and of the women who came with spices to anoint the
body of Jesus. . . .'

From such simple beginnings the plays developed into
several different kinds of drama. By the thirteenth century in
England, although continuing to be performed within the
church, plays were also being performed out-of-doors and in
the vernacular, and were no longer connected with specific
church services. The various forms of drama that developed
are known as liturgical plays, saints' plays, the mystery/
miracle cycles, morality plays and finally Tudor interludes. It
is not until the Tudor interludes, which first appear at the end
of the fifteenth century, that the element of entertainment and
professionalism in both writing and acting becomes established.

All medieval drama is didactic drama, teaching and
spreading the Christian faith, promoting the godly way of life

and condemning vice. In effect the church acknowledged that drama can be a powerful medium of propaganda, and utilised it accordingly. The playwrights were anonymous, writing for the glory of God, though clearly they must have belonged to the clergy for no one else at this time would have been sufficiently well educated or well enough versed in Christian dogma to write such plays. The plays were based on Bible stories, the lives of saints, the life, death and resurrection of Christ, vices and virtues, angels and devils, God and Satan, and were anything but dull.

Once plays had begun to be presented outside the church building in the open air, and were no longer written in Latin or tied to a church service, development was rapid. Drama continued to promote the Christian way of life, but lay actors and lay managements began to take over the presentation from the clergy. This was particularly so in the case of the great cycle plays. All plays were written in verse (prose drama does not appear until the mid-sixteenth century) and all drama continued to be 'occasional' drama, that is, presented on special occasions only and not available for daily consumption. Indeed, the cycle plays were so expensive that it was fortunate they could be performed only once a year – to celebrate the Feast of Corpus Christi; because it was open-air drama, performances were limited to spring and summer.

The performers were mainly amateurs, but this is not to say that performances were of a low standard, since records exist referring to 'cunning and discreet players'. The style of acting was probably very simple to match the simplicity of the text:

> Now cease of your talking, and give lordly audience!
> Not a word, I charge you that are here present!
> Be none so hardy to presume in my high presence
> To unloose his lips against my intent.
> I am Herod, of the Jews King most reverent.
>
> *Ludus Coventriae*

There would have been little room for subtlety when performances were given outdoors and texts were always in verse. The features of medieval acting seem to have been a loud voice (to quell the audience's chatter) and a strong physical presence to convey authority.

There has been a recent renewal of interest in medieval drama, and many people have had the opportunity to witness (or even to perform in) productions of the cycle plays at York, Chester, Coventry and Lincoln.

Less well known but quite as spectacular and perhaps even more exciting is the type of play called a morality. The most frequently quoted example is *Everyman,* but in fact it is not a typical morality play. For one thing it is humourless, and for another it does not contain any of the personified Deadly Sins such as Pride and Lechery. Much more attractive and powerful is the morality play *The Castle of Perseverance* (*c.* 1425). It tells the story of Humanum Genus (the central character representing Mankind) who is born, grows to maturity, falls into bad habits with the Seven Deadly Sins (they all appear in the play), is rescued by the Seven Virtues (all lovely ladies) with the help of Shrift and Penance, only to fall into the hands of the deadliest of the Sins, Covetousness. At this point Death stalks in unexpectedly and claims him. His soul, which devils immediately seize and carry off to Hell, is saved from eternal damnation at the eleventh hour by the intercession of four beautiful ladies, the Daughters of God, named Justice, Mercy, Peace and Truth. The play ends with God the Father and his angels appearing on Heaven/stage calling on the Soul, whom He has pardoned, to join Him and 'be exalted in bounty and bliss' for evermore. For those people who think that religious drama is dull and dutiful, here is an exciting, spectacular medieval play combining the bawdy and beautiful, the devilish and the heavenly. Although written in verse, the language is forceful and colourful. Here is some straight talk from Covetousness:

> Yah! Up and down thou take the way
>   Through this world to walk and wend,
> And thou shalt find, truth to say,
>   Thy purse shall be thy best friend.
> Though thou sit all day and pray,
>   No man shall come to thee, nor send,
> Except thou have a penny to pay. . . .

The medieval Mystery Cycle plays performed in 1981 in front of the
great West door of Lincoln Cathedral – the precise location that
would have been used in medieval times. Here, a single fixed stage is
used; in medieval times they may have employed several different
stages, or movable wagons, or even played 'in-the-round'.

the
staging
of medieval
drama

the staging of medieval drama

In the Middle Ages theatre buildings were still unknown; temporary stages were erected in convenient open-air locations and performances were given in daylight. The most usual form of outdoor staging is known as the booth stage. Pieter Breughel the Younger's painting *Flemish Fair* gives a vivid impression of how it looked and worked.

On special occasions, to celebrate a particularly important Feast Day, a bigger and more elaborate stage might be erected with free-standing scenic elements placed along its length; as for the Passion Play performed in Valenciennes, France, in 1547, meticulously recorded in a painting by Hubert Cailleau. The fearsome Hell-mouth sprouted real smoke and flame, and the boat actually sailed across real water. It was a massively spectacular production in every way.

The staging for a French Mystery play at Valenciennes in 1547.
Hell-mouth (*L'enfer*, right of picture) gushed real fire and smoke, and opened and closed.

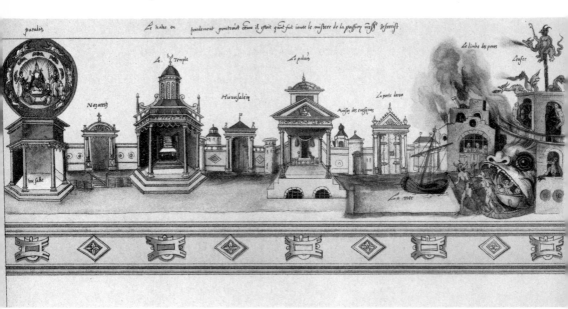

Another popular form of staging made use of specially prepared (sometimes purpose-built) farm waggons on which plays were performed. They made fine temporary stages, were transportable and eminently suited to the presentation of open-air drama. These waggons, known as pageant waggons, were used either singly or in groups; they were sometimes placed in a set arrangement on a piece of open ground, or trundled through the streets, one after the other, each waggon containing a different play, and stopping and playing at specific locations known as stations. The play's action would take place primarily on the waggon itself, but could spill over on to the street. The audience stood around in a semi-circle to watch, or were more comfortably ensconced at windows of nearby buildings. This is the method of presentation known to have been used for the performance of the York cycle plays in the fifteenth and sixteenth centuries.

By far the most exciting form of staging in medieval times is known as 'in the round' or 'place and scaffold' presentation. *The Castle of Perseverance* was written for this form of staging. (The notion of theatre in the round as a modern invention is antedated by some five hundred years!) The play's action takes place in the circular arena, and on and between the various central and perimeter stages. This kind of an arrangement enabled 'journeys' to be paced out around the arena, and several different actions to go on simultaneously — it was a unique and highly effective form of staging.

the production

Evidence has survived to show that the medieval property men were every bit as ingenious as their modern counterparts. God appeared in a burning bush; the Israelites passed safely through the Red Sea, the waters of which (large blue cloths) conveniently divided to permit safe passage, only to engulf the pursuing Egyptians moments later; and animals 'two by two' were conveyed into Noah's Ark (painted on boards or cut-outs). Scenes such as these were easily accomplished, as were the grisly tortures meted out at the martyrdom of saints.

the
production
Bladders of pig's blood beneath costumes provided realistic blood lettings, and where flaying alive or burning at the stake were necessary dummies were skilfully substituted at the last moment. A practical Hell-mouth – a prominent feature of many medieval stages – would have been lovingly constructed in the traditional shape of a huge beast's head, the jaws of which opened and closed to the accompaniment of much smoke and flame and the indispensable crackling of fireworks. Pyrotechnics were a special feature of medieval drama, not only for Hell-mouth but also to be secreted about the persons of devils. One well-known stage direction reads: 'And he that shall play Belial look that he have gunpowder burning in pipes in his hands and in his ears and in his arse when he goeth to battle.' With such attractive dramatic features it is not surprising that in time the entertainment aspect of the plays began to gain ground over religious dogma. Secular drama performed for its own sake was just round the corner.

Tudor interludes

The secular play arrives with the Tudor interlude, so called because the earliest extant examples in England come from the Tudor period. The term 'interlude' is also apt in that it suggests a shortish play, which indeed the majority were. The Tudor interlude severed all connection with religion; its purpose was essentially that of entertainment, its content secular, and its performers professionals. Interludes were presented not as the main attraction of an evening's entertainment but rather as an *hors-d'oeuvre* or something to be presented during an interval – at a banquet for instance. Outdoors at fairs and markets they were the right length to hold the attention of a crowd long enough amid other distractions. Music, song and dance were often mixed in with the 'matter of the play'.

A typical Tudor interlude is the play *The Four PP's* by John Heywood in which a Pardoner, a Palmer, a Pedlar and a 'Pothecary meet, and after extolling their own individual virtues disagree as to which is the better man. They decide to settle the issue by way of a competition – a lying competition, to see who can tell the biggest fib! It is won by the Palmer (one who indulges in pilgrimages), who starts his tale by suggesting that in all his experience he has never seen nor known

> . . . Any one woman out of patience.

Such a remark instantly renders him the victor. The play has no narrative development and little characterisation; it is simply an amusing discussion performed to pass the time away pleasantly, a sort of cabaret item. Even though a moral tone occasionally intruded, these plays were esentially performed to create mirth and pleasure:

> . . . Both good examples and right honest solace.
> This play, in like wise, I am sure
> Is made for the same intent and purpose
> To do every man both mirth and pleasure . . .

Fulgens and Lucrece, c. 1497

Interludes were simply presented, no stage being required. Indoors, they just 'took the floor' in Tudor halls or large chambers; outdoors, the booth stage was perfectly adequate.

The professional performers of interludes clearly came from the ranks of the professional entertainers, as is evident from the inclusion in these early pieces of songs, dances and physical byplay. By taking up acting they were merely adding to their skills and exploiting a medium which was fast catching on. Even though the drama had now turned secular, religious plays still continued to be performed in churches and out of doors. They remained popular throughout the fifteenth and sixteenth centuries, only ceasing to be played as a result of the Catholic–Protestant controversy following the Reformation, when they were censored out of existence.

Secular drama during this period continued to expand, and rather longer and more serious moral interludes developed from around 1500, mixing scenes of boisterous horseplay with contrasting passages of high seriousness. Acting at this time was beginning to need skills in handling dialogue and manipulating audiences, but did not yet need

Tudor interludes

profound character studies or verbal interplay. The extent of characterisation in the writing was still slight, so that no performances called for great imaginative acting. The plays consisted mainly of passages of dialogue between two people only, or at the most three or four characters, sandwiched between long solo speeches.

Five hundred years had now elapsed in England since drama re-emerged through church ritual, but a major step forward had been taken, resulting in plays professionally performed and presented solely for pleasure. Prose drama, theatre buildings, the professional playwright, regular daily performance of plays – all these had still to come. They did so in the sixteenth century.

8

THE RENAISSANCE TO THE INTERREGNUM

Renaissance drama

Two great movements, the Renaissance and the Reformation, pushed the drama firmly out of its religious mould. The Renaissance movement, through its discoveries and studies of classical Greek and Roman art, including drama, was responsible for revolutionising the content and form of drama. The Reformation's squabbles over religious issues rendered religious drama too hot to handle, leaving secular drama a clear field.

The atmosphere of study during the Renaissance made drama a subject of eager investigation by academics in mid-sixteenth-century England. It became a growth industry in Tudor institutes of learning; acting and play production were regularly practised, not for themselves alone but because they were thought beneficial to students graduating into public life, where debate and the conduct of affairs required an ability to speak in public with clarity, articulation and intelligence. As one Tudor playwright remarked: 'This [the study and practice of drama] is held necessary for the

**Renaissance
drama**

emboldening of their junior scholars to arm them with audacity [boldness] against they come to be employed in any public exercise ... it emboldens a scholar to speak, but instructs him to speak well, and with judgement.'

The first half of Queen Elizabeth's reign (1558–1603) was the 'melting-pot' period of English drama, when it refined itself, experimenting with language, form and content. It reached maturity in the hands of master craftsmen such as Shakespeare and his contemporaries near the end of her reign. It was a time when the language itself was being refined – a Golden Age of poetry as well as of drama. In the course of these language experiments plays were written in a variety of metres and verse forms, ranging from simple rhymed couplets to the jog-trot rhythms of the notorious 'four-teener' (a line of fourteen syllables). How unsuitable some of these forms were can be seen from the following example:

> As I on horseback up did leap, my sword from
> scabbard shot
> And ran me thus into the side, as you right well
> may see. . . .

> Robert Preston, *Cambyses, King of Persia, c.* 1561

Much ingenuity was shown in the verse forms employed, but eventually most playwrights settled for blank verse – unrhymed iambic pentameter. The bulk of late sixteenth- and early seventeenth-century verse drama is written in this form, pioneered mainly by Christopher Marlowe and perfected by William Shakespeare. Prose made its first appearance in drama with Gascoigne's play *Supposes*, translated from the Italian around 1566; the subsequent chief exploiter of prose was John Lyly, specifically writing for the Boy Players.

As for the form and structure of a play – whether it conformed to a strict genre such as comedy or tragedy, and whether it was structured like classical drama – English dramatists, generally uncaring, used no rules or forged their own. Classical plays had been written to a set formula which in the Renaissance period was largely interpreted as the rule of the three unities. Plays written to such a formula were termed neo-classical, i.e. the new or modern classical style.

The rule governed the time, place and action of a play: the
time span of the play should not be above twelve hours – it
should not range over a period of years, but preferably equal
the playing time of a couple of hours; the action should all
take place at the same location and not dart about all over
Europe; and the plot line should be confined to a continuous
single action and not attempt to cover several simultaneous
sub-plots. Few English dramatists persisted with the neo-
classical style, though it had great potential within such a
strict framework for producing varied and effective plays. This
was much to the regret of Sir Philip Sidney, one of the earliest
English drama critics, who complained sadly of the sprawling
lack of form in most pieces of early Elizabethan drama.
Shakespeare seldom yielded to such a strict exercise; Ben
Jonson, however, did. France alone, to an exclusive degree,
adopted the rules of neo-classical drama throughout most of
the seventeenth century.

Renaissance drama

As for subject matter, once religious drama was no
longer possible, and biblical topics and stories and religious
dogma had to be dispensed with, the world was the playwright's oyster. But it is interesting that development was
cautious. Denied the Bible for subject-matter, playwrights
turned to other books, seeking suitable stories to dramatise.
They found the chronicles and history books full of classical,
mythical and factual stories, and for a time history plays had a
tremendous vogue. They all appeared in the 1590s, and
strangely enough disappeared just as suddenly. Popular too
were plays dealing with contemporary news items like a sensational mid-sixteenth-century murder in Kent used for *Arden
of Faversham*, and the later equally dire northern happenings
described in *A Yorkshire Tragedy*. In days with no newspapers and few who could read anyway, if a playwright could
get hold of the details of a 'hot' story and quickly dramatise it
there was money to be made. Even Marlowe ventured into
this sort of play with his *Massacre at Paris*, in which he
depicted the massacre of the Huguenots on St Bartholomew's
Day and the subsequent killing of the Duc de Guise, both of
which events had occurred only a couple of decades before.
Italian and French works, such as Boccaccio's *Decameron* and
the French *Fabliaux*, were also mined for suitable stories.

**Renaissance
drama**

Renaissance drama is sharply distinguished from medieval drama in that it deals more with man's relationship with man and less with his relationship with God. Subject matter was stimulated by new knowledge and scientific discoveries which began to erode the limited frontiers of medieval knowledge. Man's present life on earth, and not a promised future life in Heaven, became the central issue of many plays, especially in the late sixteenth and early seventeenth centuries. The revelations in astronomy by scientists like Copernicus, Kepler and Galileo, which the church attempted to suppress, produced a new philosophy which, as the poet John Donne remarked, 'casts all in doubt'. The most profound discovery was that the earth was no longer at the centre of the universe; the earth revolved around the sun – not, as had previously been believed, the sun around the earth. If the earth was no longer at the centre of the universe, then man was after all not God's prime creation, since he did not occupy the centre of His world. Banished to a planet revolving in space, of what importance then is this creature man? This clearly accounts in part for the 'darker side' of many late Elizabethan and Jacobean tragedies, especially in the early seventeenth century.

In a similar way comedy reflected contemporary events – though ones of less significance. There is, for instance, a genre known as citizen comedy, highlighting the growth of the monied merchant class and the decline of the hard-up aristocracy, in which the scramble to acquire money and status left grace and good manners in the dust. The plays of this period are shot through with vivid reflection – from simple references to the New Found Lands (the discovery of the Americas) to the new craze for smoking tobacco, the frivolities of fashion and experiments in alchemy.

Renaissance drama is also different from earlier drama in that it often requires interpretation. Religious medieval drama did not; being didactic, it was deliberately kept simple in order to be readily understood. But with the growth of drama, and the move away from familiar material and familiar structures, late Renaissance plays became complex; they were no longer pure narrative (telling a simple tale), but a story holding significance through analogy. For example, one of the earliest English tragedies, *Gorboduc* by Norton and Sackville, belies its simple King Lear-like tale in which a king during his own lifetime divides his realm between his two sons, which leads to a series of disasters involving the murder of the sons, the death of the queen, the deposition and death of the king himself, and violent revolution in the kingdom. Its significance is that of a cautionary tale to remind Elizabeth, a monarch and as yet unmarried, that a kingdom without an heir is an unsettled one inviting disaster. Similarly, Marlowe's play *Dr Faustus* is not merely the story of a scholar who failed to repent his sins and ended up in Hell, but a play which seems to question established religious beliefs. With Renaissance drama came drama requiring elucidation; the viewer no longer asked simply 'What happened next?' but 'Why did it happen and what can be learnt from it?'

Renaissance drama

major Renaissance playwrights

The first playwright to cause any real stir in English theatre was Christopher Marlowe (1564–93). Poet, spy, atheist, homosexual, his plays are as controversial and violent as his own death (he was killed in a tavern brawl). But he had a way with words and his plays are constantly revived today, especially *Dr Faustus*. Marlowe was an exact contemporary of Shakespeare and these two, together with Ben Jonson (1572–1637), famous for his comedies, created a formidable trio – a trio whose combined qualities have never been surpassed.

This was a period when multi-authorship was common. With a surge of interest in the theatre and because of the custom of presenting a different play each day, there was a great demand for new work. Several writers would work together, often writing an Act each. Thomas Heywood, for instance, declared that he had had a hand in nearly 220 plays, and even Ben Jonson was not averse to this procedure. The prolific output of certain Renaissance playwrights is astounding (if one credits their own statements): the Spanish playwright Lope de Vega (1562–1625) is said to have written some 2,000 plays, of which at least 470 have survived.

This was also the age of plagiarism; find something

interesting and then make it your own! Even Shakespeare borrowed most of his plots from other people's work.

As late as the end of the sixteenth century, when theatre became a commercial venture, plays were often printed and put on sale without mentioning the name of the playwright. However, if a play became a bestseller and was found to be the work of a particular playwright, it became the practice to include that playwright's name; certain unscrupulous printers, hoping for good sales, did not hesitate to put Shakespeare's name to plays of which he was *not* the author.

William Shakespeare

Shakespeare (1564–1616) really deserves a chapter of his own. Sadly, though, many people find him unapproachable – they consider him too heavyweight, or too historical without relevance to modern life; they find his language difficult to penetrate; and perhaps, like many of us, they suffered from unimaginative teaching and force-feeding of the so-called 'classics' when they were at school, and have reacted against that ever since. But – with the exception of the last of these complaints – nothing could be further from the truth. Shakespeare was a giant among playwrights, standing head and shoulders above his contemporaries, talented though they were, and way above most of his predecessors and successors too.

But *why* was he so great? The answer is that he managed to combine brilliant characterisation, incomparable mastery of verse, and a deep understanding of human nature in a way that no one else could. His plots were not original – it was what he did with them that was so unique.

While Shakespeare's plays are as full as any of his fellow playwrights' with comment on contemporary events, the substance of his plays has more lasting significance. When celebrating the potential majesty of Renaissance man, Shakespeare also draws attention to his weaknesses, as in the following two passages from *Hamlet* and *Henry VIII*.

What a piece of work is man! how noble in reason!
how infinite in faculty! in form and moving how
express and admirable! in action, how like an angel!
in apprehension, how like a God! the beauty of the
world, the paragon of animals. . . .

**William
Shakespeare**

. . . but we all are men,
In our own natures frail . . . few are angels.

He sighs deeply for man's frequent fall from grace – the frailty
of nature, the flesh that pulls him down. Again and again
throughout his work Shakespeare draws attention to man's
need for self-control; he shows that by surrendering to
immediate responses and passions – particularly those of
anger, desire, ambition, jealousy and revenge – the result
ultimately is only destructive.

This philosophy is summed up by Hamlet when
speaking to Horatio. 'Give me that man,' he says 'that is not
passion's slave, and I will wear him in my heart's core – ay, in
my heart of hearts, as I do thee, Horatio.' In the play, Horatio
proves his only friend. Hamlet refers to him as the ideal
balanced individual:

As one, in suffering all, that suffers nothing.
A man that fortune's buffets and rewards
Hast ta'en with equal thanks; and blest are those
Whose blood and judgement are so well commingled
That they are not a pipe for fortune's finger
To sound what stop she please.

In other words he has a balanced disposition: he is neither
instantly depressed by bad news, nor deliriously happy the
moment good fortune smiles on him. He is constant, able to
adjust to good and bad times, never allowing his feelings to
run away with him. Shakespeare's 'messages' – of which this
is but one example – have at least as much relevance to late
twentieth-century man as they did four centuries ago.

Unlike a number of famous playwrights, who restrict
themselves to a single genre, Shakespeare explored almost
the whole range of drama – comedies, tragedies, history plays,
dark comedies and the later non-naturalistic drama known as

William Shakespeare

the romance plays. In all he wrote some thirty-seven plays as well as poetry, and even in his own day he was acknowledged as far outshining his fellow playwrights.

His work falls into several quite clearly defined periods as indicated below, suggesting a progression of maturity and a developing philosophy of life. Though some of these periods overlap and there is no universal agreement on the dating of the plays, a pattern emerges.

1591–99	History plays
1592–95	Early comedies
1596–99	Major comedies
1600–06	Major tragedies
1602–07	Dark comedies
1608–11	Romances

His plays are remarkable in their objectivity – his own personality does not obtrude. Even from such a vast output it is difficult to discern beneath the plays Shakespeare's own persona. Marlowe's plays reflect his personality and interests quite clearly – his classical learning, his delight in the 'mighty line' of dramatic verse poetry, his leanings towards homosexuality, his straining after knowledge – and give a picture of an ardent and active Renaissance scholar questioning previously accepted concepts about religion, the world, and life after death. Ben Jonson exhibits his classical learning too, but this time in respect of dramatic form and shape. Jonson is revealed as a precise, moral individual, who believed that plays should be 'pleasure with instruction' instruments, teaching man how he ought to live. He is proud of his scholarship (largely self-taught) and anxious to display it. But behind Shakespeare's plays, the man himself lies unrevealed – though, as indicated above, he clearly held certain principles.

He began by writing history plays and broad comedies of a light-hearted nature, plays which already showed his ability to deal with a large number of characters and a fairly complicated plot line. He adroitly used blank verse and prose, and indulged in linguistic tricks, such as plays on words, especially in the roles he created for his fools and clowns, so beloved of contemporary audiences. Throughout the 1590s he was engaged in completing his sequence of history plays. The genre had a tremendous vogue at this time which resulted in some excellent narrative plays dealing with the life and death, bloody battles and squabbles over the throne, of a number of English kings. Though in many instances Shakespeare distorted historical fact, he none the less gave a vivid account of English history from the late fourteenth century up to his own day. The achievement is all the more remarkable in that the plays were not written chronologically. He took his facts from the several Chronicles published in his time, adapting them as he saw fit. Read as a group, these history plays indicate that, whichever king was occupying the throne, the real protagonist was England herself, and the plays comment on the nature of the relationship between king and country.

William Shakespeare

Also in the 1590s, Shakespeare turned his attention to mature comedy, writing such plays as *The Merchant of Venice, As You Like It* and *Twelfth Night,* in which he seems to celebrate the power of love and the strength and qualities of his female characters. Portia, Rosalind and Viola possess great resilience to misfortune, embodying a positive force and attitude to life which enables them ultimately to win through and achieve their desires. A definition of comedy in academic terms suggests that it begins in disharmony and ends in harmony, often with a marriage betrothal or nuptial celebrations as a symbol of such harmony. Shakespeare builds on this, highlighting the necessity for fortitude in adversity and the positive power of love.

By 1600 he had moved into the period of his great tragedies – *Hamlet, King Lear, Othello* and *Macbeth* were all written by 1606. Even as he completed the history plays he was becoming more and more interested in the nature of the individual monarch and his private thoughts – as opposed to the public deeds that make up the tale of a monarch's reign. Thus stimulated, he moved on to the complex psychological studies found in the great tragedies in which he probes the thoughts and conflicts of the mind and the stresses and strains to which an individual is subject throughout his life. This

**William
Shakespeare**

interest can be seen coming to the fore in Shakespeare's early treatment of a monarch, King Richard III – the hunchback king who reputedly murdered the Princes in the Tower among others in his bloody progress to the throne. This particular play seems to move away from the stuff of history to concern itself with the stuff of tragedy when, towards the close of the play, Richard's conscience – hitherto totally suppressed – suddenly surfaces and utterly destroys his composure. Richard wakes uneasily from a nightmare in which the ghosts of all the people he has murdered visit him to curse and denounce him, foretelling that the following day's battle (Bosworth Field) will prove disastrous. In this play the self-analysis occurs somewhat abruptly, but in the later tragedies Shakespeare's technique becomes more sophisticated and he takes us step by step along the terrible downward paths that Lear, Othello and Macbeth tread. We not only experience with them the full extent of their anguish, but are shown how and perhaps why things happened as they did.

At this time Shakespeare seems to have become concerned with what might be termed the darker side of life. Soon after turning his attention to the tragedies he wrote what have become known as the dark comedies – *Measure for Measure, Troilus and Cressida* and *Timon of Athens,* in which a mood of gloom, disillusionment and despair at man's behaviour colours the plays and evokes a saddened response. The corrupting nature of power and lust is shown in *Measure for Measure;* love tarnishes and is destroyed in *Troilus and Cressida;* while the grasping nature of man and his ingratitude are exposed in *Timon of Athens.*

The final phase of Shakespeare's work produced plays markedly different both in form and content from any of his earlier work. Known as the romance plays, they provide an overview of life from the vantage-point of maturity and with a serene optimism. Time is seen as a healing agent, helping to mend the torn fabric of life. The plays are set in strange and remote lands; the plots have an almost fairy-tale quality; and the action is often more symbolic than naturalistic. Time is an important element, for the plays' action covers a period long enough for lost children to be restored (grown to marriageable age) and for betrothals to be announced which unite previously estranged families or parents. *Pericles, The Winter's Tale, Cymbeline* and *The Tempest* are plays of this kind.

All Shakespeare's work is written in verse and prose of incomparable quality and is brought to life on stage by a succession of vivid characters which have become household names – Falstaff, Hamlet, Portia, Macbeth, Viola, Shylock and Bottom. The language may be of the sixteenth and seventeenth centuries, but the sentiments expressed are 'not of an age, but for all time'. To experience in the theatre a fine production of any of his major plays is to be in touch with the very pulse of life and to be provided with many 'imperishable moments'.

Jacobean drama

By the time James I had inherited the English crown in 1603 dramatists were becoming concerned with man's inhumanity to man and the susceptibility of human nature to succumb to evil or to be depressed by the cares of life. Jacobean drama generally has an air of disillusionment and scepticism. Spiritual despondency is often the keynote, and as T. S. Eliot remarks of one particular playwright, 'He is much concerned with death.' As the century unfolds, so do the plays of corrupt courts, vicious behaviour and vengeful intrigue, such as *The Duchess of Malfi* by Webster and *The Atheist's Tragedy* by Tourneur. Such plays stand in marked contrast with the preceding Elizabethan drama where the accent is on man's positive virtues: the aspirations of Marlowe's heroes, for instance, the qualities of leadership and statesmanship displayed in the history plays, the virtuous heroes of classical legend and romantic tales which formed the plots of earlier plays.

Caroline drama

By the Caroline period the drama had changed even further. After 1625, when Charles I came to the throne, disillusionment and the lack of answers to radical questions resulted in a

period of resigned acceptance or a mood of escapism. This trend is clearly marked in the drama by the emergence of a much greater number of tragi-comedies – plays in which tragedy is hinted at but never actually arrives: 'There is the danger but not the death.' The very nature of playwriting underwent a change and it became a dilettante occupation, no longer the province of a flourishing professional body of writers but the sphere of the gentleman amateur, the educated man wishing to be thought the complete man of letters. There were few dedicated professional playwrights working in the Caroline period; notable exceptions were John Ford and James Shirley.

Caroline drama

The attitude to a once serious drama is now apparent in the work of, for example, Sir John Suckling, who wrote a play called *Aglaura* for which he provided two fifth Acts so that the piece might be played as either a comedy or a tragedy, dependent on which of the two endings was chosen! The plays of the 1620s and 1630s are often characterised by shallow thinking and shallow theatricality. Such work, in fact, heralds the brittle drama of the Restoration period, heavily concerned with amorous intrigue and the behaviour of the fashionable set, and peppered with artificial and witty repartee. In short, the drama was in danger of losing its objectivity and declining into mere diversion.

Politically, the theatre was not helped by growing Puritan opposition and the decreasing power of the court and monarch to protect it. Once the court tottered, the drama too, began to falter. Theatre was eventually completely suppressed in 1642 when the Puritan Parliament began to assume total authority, later deposing Charles I; Parliament closed down all public theatres and playhouses, which remained shut during the Interregnum – a break of some eighteen years.

Opposite: A scene from Webster's *The White Devil* in the National Theatre's 1969 production, with Geraldine McEwan.

Renaissance
theatre
buildings

Renaissance theatre buildings

In terms of theatre history the Elizabethan and Jacobean period is of immense importance. In 1576 the first English permanent playhouse building was erected. Called the Theater, it was located in what is now Bishopsgate in London. It was closely followed by another called the Curtain in 1577, and then by others on the south bank of the Thames. Called playhouses rather than theatres, they housed not plays exclusively, but other 'play' activity such as sword and fencing bouts, dancing and singing, feats of juggling, tumbling, acrobatics and the like. The shape of the playhouse was that of the contemporary bull- or bear-baiting houses, a three-storey polygon-shaped building surrounding a central, almost circular, area open to the skies. A stage was built at ground level against one side of the galleries and jutted out half-way into the pit. It was not until 1599 that the first purpose-built theatre was erected expressly for the performance of plays; this was the Globe, built on Bankside not far from the site of today's National Theatre. The drama now settled down, continued to develop and soon established itself as an everyday activity. It had come of age. Educated young men, introduced to drama during their student days and now wishing to earn a living by their pens, found that theatre could provide a livelihood – the professional playwright made his first entrance and with him came the theatrical impresario and commercial theatre.

However, the drama did not proceed without opposition. Although it was firmly supported by Queen Elizabeth, her court and the aristocracy generally, the City of London authorities greatly disliked it and took active steps to ban it. As a result all London playhouses were built outside the City limits, beyond its immediate jurisdiction, with sites in north London and more popularly on the south bank. Plays were also performed on temporary stages set up in inn yards. All this activity took place in the open air and was therefore not possible at night or during the late autumn and winter. Performances at court, in institutions of learning or in the halls of the nobility were of course indoor performances (and private

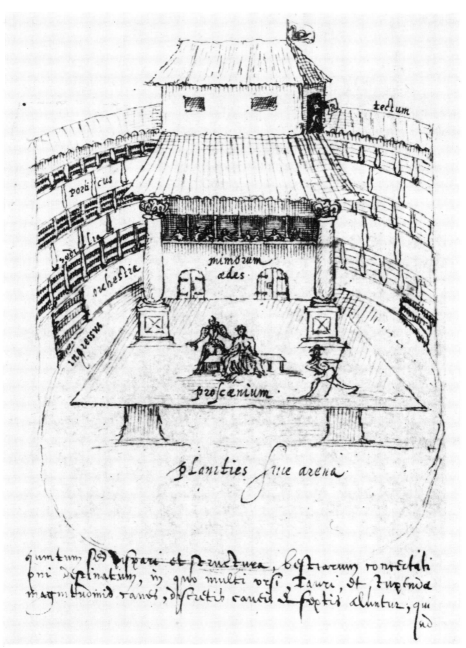

The only contemporary pictorial evidence of the interior of an
Elizabethan playhouse – the de Witt sketch of the Swan Theatre,
1596.

Renaissance theatre buildings

ones), but the bulk of all public dramatic activity took place out of doors.

In James I's reign the tradition of the so-called 'private' indoor playhouses began. Not that admittance to such theatres was in any way restricted; the only condition of entry was the depth of your purse, for they were much more expensive than the outdoor public playhouses and therefore attracted a different class of audience. Since they were indoor theatres the type of play and its manner of presentation were subtly affected. A more 'masque-like' form of drama was possible, influenced by the sumptuous court masques, devised by Inigo Jones and Ben Jonson, presented at James' court. With an enclosed stage and auditorium a more intimate, less declamatory style of acting was possible. The most notable indoor theatre was the Blackfriars, which occupied a site close to that of today's Mermaid Theatre at Puddle Dock.

There was no scenery in the modern sense in either the public or the private theatres. Although scenery in the Italian theatre during this period had progressed enormously, particularly with the adoption of perspective-painted flats, these were unknown on the English stage – although Inigo Jones had introduced them into the masques at court. Scenery in playhouses and theatres was emblematic, offering a token only, such as a bed to represent a bedroom, a throne to represent the court, a single tree for a forest, or a small mound to represent a mountain. More often than not the actors would play against the background of the stage architecture, varied perhaps with a hanging tapestry or curtain, but in no sense was any effort expended to make the stage resemble a specific setting. Indeed, the 'unlocalised' stage of the Elizabethan and Jacobean period was one of its chief assets, enabling scene after scene to follow quickly without having to pause for scenery to be changed or added.

What such theatres lacked in scenery, however, they made up for with costumes. Visitors to London attending the playhouse left many descriptions and comments about the gorgeous nature of the players' garb. Such wardrobes were mainly based on contemporary fashions, for it appears that Renaissance theatre had little sense of historical accuracy in the costuming of its plays.

From Shakespeare's *Hamlet* (the Prince's advice to the players) it is clear that acting has become a formal art. The actor is told to suit 'the action to the word, the word to the action', suggesting that acting was probably fairly static, more vocal than physical, the prime requisite being a strong, eloquent and persuasive speaking voice. A considerable amount of sixteenth-century drama describes rather than permits its plots to be acted out. This form of poetic verse drama is ideal therefore for 'pronunciation' in its delivery; it rouses the audience's imagination – vastly different from today's more physical performances.

Renaissance theatre buildings

1642–60: the interregnum

With the closure of all theatres in 1642, the presentation of plays to the public ceased. Theatre was eclipsed by a greater drama of real life played out between king and country, which culminated on a public scaffold with the execution of Charles I in 1649. England became a Commonwealth and was governed by a largely Puritan government whose way of life included nothing so frivolous as plays. With the Restoration of the monarchy under Charles II in 1660, theatres once more opened their doors. What they revealed was a vastly altered stage and auditorium, for the drama had retreated indoors; there was scenery on stage, seats in the pit and actresses waiting in the wings.

9

RESTORATION AND THE EIGHTEENTH CENTURY

After the enforced gap of eighteen years during the Interregnum, when theatre resumed it had almost to make a fresh beginning. Few trained actors were available, none of the previous theatre buildings was intact, and a whole generation was alive who had never seen a play! Expertise, however, was still available. On assuming the throne Charles II licensed only two individuals to open theatres, creating a monopoly which plagued succeeding theatrical impresarios and managers for a century and a half. Sir William Davenant and Thomas Killigrew were given the exclusive right to present plays. Both began with makeshift theatres adapted from indoor tennis courts until purpose-built theatres became available; they were dubbed the 'patent houses', since they alone had letters-patent to present plays.

Davenant, with his company called the Duke's Men, early introduced scenery and theatrical machinery into his theatre, while Killigrew with his King's Men opened without scenery but was forced to follow suit when the new concept of staging instantly caught on. It may seem surprising that Restoration London, with a population greater than that during the Commonwealth, could support only two theatres when more that half a dozen had flourished less than fifty years before. Audiences, however, were not as numerous as they had been (the theatre-going habit had died), and during the early years of the Restoration theatre, functioned very much as a club for the privileged few. The king and his court visited it, and it was patronised by the rich and leisured classes; but even though it is incorrect to say that the theatre attracted only the upper classes, few workaday people attended. It depended, however, on the season. Samuel Pepys, whose famous *Diary* reveals a great deal about the Restoration stage, comments that on one of his visits the house was full of Parliamentmen 'as a result of a holiday for them', and that on another occasion it was 'full of citizens and so the less pleasant'; though he delighted when he found the house 'full of a great company' graced by Charles II and his friends, and notably the 'very fine ladies'.

When the two theatres first opened, they presented plays written in the early part of the century by such playwrights as Shakespeare and Jonson, suitably adapted, but the most popular dramatists were Beaumont and Fletcher. Once new playwrights had begun writing for the stage, three main kinds of drama appeared, reflecting contemporary trends in social tastes and morals: comedies of manners, heroic tragedy and musical dramas. The quality and significance of early seventeenth-century drama was not generally recaptured.

The Restoration comedy of manners has often been attacked as valueless and unimportant, not being thought worthy of serious attention. But this is a superficial comment. In spite of the fact that most of these comedies are restricted almost exclusively to casts of leisured aristocrats and the upper classes, apparently wasting their days in the never-ending pursuit of social and sexual pleasure, the plays merit further consideration. Thackeray characterised it as 'that miserable, rouged, tawdry, sparkling, hollow-hearted comedy . . .' and certainly many such characters and situations exist in the plays – their very cast lists proclaim it: Sir Fopling Flutter, Sir Novelty Fashion, Mr Tattle and Mr Scandal; Lady Cockwood, Mrs Squeamish, Miss Hoyden. A closer look at the plays, however, reveals substance behind the hypocrisy and sniggers.

In every Restoration comedy there is usually a serious, sensible pair of lovers, often kept apart by circumstances or by jealous parents who plan to marry them off elsewhere. Such genuine lovers contrast with the glittering veneer of the 'rouged and tawdry', indicating that beneath the tinkling pleasantries of a self-centred society can be found true emotion and sensibility. Moreover, many of the rakes who flit desperately from mistress to mistress, have, before the play is done, become tired of the sexual merry-go-round and found someone of whom they are genuinely fond. The major pre-occupations of playwrights with failed marriages, extra-marital sex, the pursuit of love and intrigue reflect a society in which upper-class marriages were seldom love matches but arranged marriages of convenience which often brought together couples between whom there could be little sympathy. In such cases sexual satisfaction could only be gained outside marriage. As a contemporary satire remarked:

> For Matrimony's but a bargain made
> To serve the Turne of Interest and Trade,
> Not out of Love or Kindness, but designs
> To settle Land and Tenements like Fines.

The accent on marriage is clear in such titles as *The Provok'd Wife* and *The Relapse*, but it is not the sacrament of marriage itself which is being attacked, only the contemporary attitude towards it. The position of divorce and marriage in the late seventeenth century is also being highlighted. In arranged marriages, the divorce of incompatible partners was not only out of the question because of the vested interests of one or both partners, but was unobtainable without a dispensation from Parliament. What such plays emphasise is the discrepancy between appearance and reality – the hollowness and pretence which requires society to keep up appearances when the actuality is so corrupt. Such drama is a clear reflection of late seventeenth-century high society – we may tolerate the deceit and dissimulation or detest it, but a good production of a fine Restoration comedy will prove a thoroughly enjoyable theatrical experience, for many of the plays are highly amusing, witty and ingenious.

The Restoration romp *The Country Wife* by William Wycherley, with
Albert Finney and Elizabeth Spriggs at the National Theatre, 1977.

The Country Wife by William Wycherley is probably the most frequently revived play from this period, depicting as it does the contemporary sexual merry-go-round. The famous 'china scene' in which, under the innocent guise of collecting rare china assignations are made and relationships are consummated, is wickedly funny.

Heroic tragedy is less acceptable to modern taste. Composed mainly in rhymed couplets, it is impossibly artificial, full of high sentiment in situations concerned with love, honour and duty. John Dryden and Sir Robert Howard appear to have written the first such tragedy, *The Indian Queen* (1663), and Dryden contributed several more, all of which were very fashionable and enthusiastically received. Of less rarified tragedy there is a dearth; one of the best is *Venice Preserved* (1682) by Thomas Otway.

Musical dramas were also very much in vogue during this period, though less often performed because of the high cost of production. Thomas Shadwell's *Psyche* (1675) and Charles Davenent's *Circe* (1677) established the form. They are important because they show a growing interest in an English theatre of music, which later develops into dramatic opera and became extremely popular in the eighteenth century. This reflects the interest in opera in Italy which had established the genre earlier in the seventeenth century.

Restoration theatre buildings

Being indoors, the design of theatre buildings in the Restoration period was very different from its previous open-air counterpart. The building itself was rectangular with a fan-shaped auditorium. The stage had a deep fore-stage, flanked on either side of the proscenium arch by pairs of doors (usually two pairs) which gave access to the stage. Acting took place on this fore-stage, behind which was an inner stage primarily intended as a scenic stage. Within this scenic area shutters in grooves, and hanging cloths, gave a painted representation of the desired setting. Mechanical means existed to change the picture into an alternative setting within seconds. Flying machinery was also installed, which produced startling illusions and enabled the rapid ascent or descent of small scenic units such as cloud formations or sky chariots, as well as the 'flying' of actors. Such effects were primarily used in heroic tragedy and operatic presentations. The auditorium was intimate, with the area directly in front of the stage (the pit) filled with rows of backless wooden benches covered in a green cloth. The wits and beaux and occasionally ladies sat in the pit, though it was more usual for ladies to take their place in the tiered boxes; certainly older persons of quality sat there. The gallery was mainly occupied by servants, footmen and the like. Illumination was by candlelight, and the auditorium remained lit during the performance.

The two newly built 'patent' houses were the Theatre Royal, Drury Lane, 1663, and the Dorset Garden Theatre, 1671. The capacity of these early theatres is not known for certain, but it is estimated that seating could cope comfortably with no more than a few hundred. Later theatres pushed the capacity up to five hundred or more.

Actresses were now beginning to play the female parts as boy actors were gradually being dispensed with, so acting must certainly have been freer, particularly as many plays, especially comedy, forsook verse and were written in prose. However the Restoration stage, though now using scenery, was in no sense a naturalistic one – doors, windows, objects and furniture were still only painted on canvas flats. Acting was still largely a matter of fine speaking and the ability to wear fine clothes.

Whatever you may think of Restoration drama as a whole, the period is important for the creation of the theatre monopoly, the introduction of actresses and the first female professional playwright (Aphra Behn), the newly designed indoor theatres with their scenes and machines, and the greatly increased use of music, much of it by Henry Purcell.

eighteenth-century drama

Good Queen Anne, the last of the Stuarts, reigned from 1702 to 1714, and was followed by the first sovereign of the House of Hanover, George I. The tone of the drama tended to be as staid as the monarchy. In spite of the eminent actor David Garrick, whose work spans this century, and in spite of a number of plays containing political fireworks, plus a few sparkling plays in the 1770s by Richard Brinsley Sheridan and Sir Oliver Goldsmith, the eighteenth century was not an outstanding one in terms of theatre.

Drama at the beginning of the century is labelled 'sentimental' (meaning full of sentiment): it is pious, moralistic, elegant but rather dull. By 1700 Restoration drama had clearly toned itself down. Congreve's *The Way of the World* (1700) and Farquhar's two plays *The Recruiting Officer* and *The Beaux' Stratagem* (1706 and 1707) have none of the hallmarks of the earlier racy comedies of manners. Farquhar in fact deserted the ladies of quality, the fops and wits of high society in London Town for a breath of country air and for characters leading a less artificial way of life. Perhaps the solid morality of Queen Anne's court, or perhaps Jeremy Collier's 1698 broadside against the libertine Restoration drama, entitled *A Short View of the Immorality and Profaneness of the English Stage* (it is anything but short), was having some effect. Whatever the reason, the pendulum was swinging the other way. Certainly the drama changed, becoming more 'decent', it is true, yet in the process perhaps becoming less witty, less attractive. Scholars and literary figures such as Sir John Addison and Dr Johnson turned their hand to playwriting now that the stage was becoming more respectable, but though their plays may have been remarked at the time they were almost instantly forgotten as declamation which 'roar'd while Passion slept'.

The two patent houses continued to exercise their monopoly despite protest from other theatrical managers wishing to present legitimate drama (as opposed to musicals). Indeed, the monopoly was confirmed more strongly than ever when, after certain plays had been performed that contained considerable political satire against the government of Sir Robert Walpole, the Prime Minister, unable privately to prevent their presentation, resorted to law. The Theatre Licensing Act of 1737 confirmed the monopoly of the two patent houses as well as instituting an effective form of

The Beggar's Opera Burlesqued, questionably attributed to Hogarth,
1728, which seems to mock both Gay's ballad opera and Italian opera
(shown on right) with the winged figure of Harmony flying away.
The scroll reads 'ready to sing and answer for verse'.

censorship. By this time the two 'legitimate' houses were the
Theatre Royal, Drury Lane (the third such theatre on this site)
and Covent Garden Theatre, built in 1732. A major theatre,
the Queen's in the Haymarket, had been built in 1705 and
intended as the second patent house, but had proved
acoustically unsuitable for drama even after alteration; it then
became exclusively devoted to opera. Musical appreciation
and love of opera grew as the eighteenth century progressed,
and Italian opera singers found ready favour in London.
Because of the monopoly, a large number of music dramas or
plays with music were presented; one of these became the
smash hit of all time – John Gay's *The Beggar's Opera,*

produced in 1728, by John Rich. The production coined a phrase quoted by everyone: 'It made Rich gay and Gay rich.'

One early eighteenth-century play entered theatre history as being the first bourgeois tragedy – John Lillo's *The London Merchant*. But the effort was not sustained, and this play remains an isolated example of serious drama at this time.

A further innovation in contemporary theatre was the presentation of an 'after-piece'. Initially this was an extra item or two of singing and dancing added to an evening's bill after the main play, but it developed into the presentation of a short comedy or farce in an effort to attract more latecomers. Performances in the early 1700s began around six o'clock, somewhat early for many people who, however, took advantage of a half-price late admission scheme. The after-piece was played to encourage them to attend, and became a regular part of an evening's programme.

After the middle of the century the theatre began to attract more and more people, mainly from the middle and lower classes. Provincial Theatre Royals were built, licensed from London to present 'legitimate' drama; two of them are still in operation today – at Bristol and at Richmond, Yorkshire. Other provincial theatres followed and by the end of the century most towns of any note had their Theatre Royal. London, too, although still limited to the two patent houses for straight drama, saw a spate of building in the 1760s with such theatres as Astley's, the Royal Circus, the Lyceum, the Pantheon and the Royalty, offering such 'non-legitimate drama' as music drama and circus drama.

eighteenth-century theatres

The physical layout of the stage gradually altered at this time; the fore-stage decreased in size as the scenic stage increased. By around 1800, the fore-stage had been reduced considerably and the scenic stage had taken over as the stage proper, so that most acting was now contained within it. Scenery and machines grew more important and complex, stages being fitted with several trap doors, bridges, fly galleries, machinery for raising and lowering scenic pieces through the stage floor (flaps) and also for flying them from above the stage. By the 1790s both Drury Lane and Covent Garden Theatres had been so patched, amended and enlarged that it was clear that new theatres had to be built. In 1792 a new Covent Garden Theatre arose, and in 1794 a new Drury Lane Theatre Royal opened its doors. In the auditoria of both theatres the pit was now surrounded by three semi-circles of tiered boxes above which was a spacious gallery. The capacity of both houses was now just over three thousand. In such huge buildings, intimate theatre was impossible; spectacle began to assume importance.

eighteenth-century theatres

By the early eighteenth century acting had acquired a traditional style and a large number of conventions. The voice was seldom modulated and actors spoke in a strange, unnatural pitch which was thought of as the correct acting tone. Marked physical postures were adopted at climactic moments, so that the cast might often look as though they were playing at statues! It was David Garrick in the 1750s who strove to move away from this long-favoured, artificial, oratorical style of acting and to give a performance that sought to convince his audience of an authentic character.

David Garrick (1717–79), actor, playwright and theatre manager, dominates the eighteenth-century stage. Of only slight physical stature, he was nevertheless a powerful figure in the theatre. His first great success was in 1741 as Richard III, and from then until his retirement in 1776 he was a radical force in the theatre. He was instrumental in improving theatrical conditions on several counts. He improved stage lighting, introduced footlights and got rid of the huge candle chandeliers which had hitherto hung over the stage, replacing them with vertical stands for lights, complete with reflectors, placed behind the proscenium arch. Candles and floating wicks in oil continued to provide the means of illumination. Perhaps one of his greatest achievements was that he finally managed to banish spectators from sitting on the stage at performances, a practice which had been going on since Elizabethan times and which Charles II had unsuccessfully attempted to curb. Garrick was also influential in attempting to establish more historically accurate costumes for period

**eighteenth-
century
theatres**

plays. At the time it was still the practice to dress all plays, no matter what the period, in contemporary high fashion; powdered wig, jacket, breeches and stockings for the men, and huge wigs and panniered skirts for the ladies. Garrick, together with another well-known actor, Charles Macklin, did much to popularise a more appropriate costume for period plays, though the practice was not to become universally followed until the early 1800s.

10

THE NINETEENTH CENTURY

Fire, a notable theatrical hazard, destroyed both patent houses early in 1800; although both theatres were soon rebuilt, the undistinguished dramatic fare continued. Indeed, the patent theatres were now so large, with capacities approaching the 3500 mark, that spectacle alone became satisfactory on stages remote from the majority of the audience. Richard Cumberland in his *Memoirs* (London, 1806) comments:

> Since the stages of Drury Lane and Covent Garden have been so enlarged in their dimensions as to be henceforward theatres for spectators rather than playhouses for hearers, it is hardly to be wondered at if their managers and directors encourage those representations to which their structure is best adapted. The splendour of the scene, the ingenuity of the machinist and the rich display of dresses, aided by the captivating charms of music now in a great degree supersede the labours of the poet. There can be nothing very gratifying in watching the movements of an actor's lips, when we cannot hear the words that proceed from them. . . .

Audiences attracted to these theatres came not for the plays but for the spectacle and such stars as John Philip Kemble, Edmund Kean, William Macready, and the greatest tragedienne of her age, Sarah Siddons. Due to the unsuitability of the two patent houses for straight drama and because of lack of financial incentive to authors, new playwrights did not appear. Such plays as were presented, like those of Shakespeare and the classics, came dressed in splendid scenery and an adulterated and cut text. Programmes were long. Triple bills were usual, with a curtain raiser, main play and a speciality item or second play.

Opera continued to be popular, and at the non-patent theatres for those of lighter musical tastes there were burlettas, burlesques and extravaganzas, all containing music and song and often interspersed with acrobats, performing animals or an exhibition of freaks. Certain theatres specialised in particular forms of entertainment; Astley's in pantomime and equestrian shows, Sadler's Wells in aquatic spectaculars. Audiences were mainly working- and lower-class; the upper classes at the beginning of the 1800s went to the opera and the two patent houses, but not elsewhere, and only the 'fast' and the more adventurous of the middle classes went to the 'illegitimate' theatres. On the whole, polite society did not patronise the theatre in the early part of the century and it was socially ostracised. Not only was the fare offered not to their liking, but the theatres were hot and uncomfortable and the audiences often unruly. Charles Dickens reported that the audience at a performance at Sadler's Wells in 1840 behaved so abominably that the place resembled a bear-garden. As if this were not enough, it was objected that loose women inhabited the theatres, soliciting customers.

Two important events in the history of the theatre occurred in the early decades of 1800. Gas lighting was introduced, and the much resented monopoly of the two patent theatres was broken.

Gas lighting gave better illumination, its intensity was easily controlled from a master valve, and it could be made directional. Its adoption led to an increased interest in scene painting, for the scenery was now much more clearly visible. Gas was introduced as early as 1817, but it was not until the

From 1804 onwards Sadler's Wells theatre became the home of
aquatic drama; a large tank was installed and filled from the New
River. Note the waterfall, riding boat and Neptune's sea-chariot.

1850s that installations were safe and advanced enough to be
generally employed. An incidental result of the ability to
control lighting led to the general practice of dimming the
houselights during the performance, thus directing the audience's concentration on to the stage. The promotion of elaborate sets and fine scene painting continued to mount
throughout the century, and certain scenic artists became
almost as celebrated as famous actors.

The breaking of the monopoly of the patent houses by the passing of the 1843 Theatre Regulatory Act was welcomed by almost everyone. It had been long overdue, and it paved the way for the drama to recover its lost eminence. But there was no immediate reaction: it took time for serious drama to reassert itself; plays and casts had to be found and trained, audiences had to be weaned away from musical shows and variety entertainments, and, above all, authors encouraged to become playwrights. The only plays which were readily available were of the melodramatic kind (presented without music now), with strong plots and striking action but of little significance. Gradually, however, through the decades that followed, plays containing attractive plots and dialogue and, indeed, offering some reflection on contemporary society began to emerge.

With few such new plays readily available, the demand for straight plays after 1843 was met from France, for it was easier and quicker to translate a play than to compose one. It was also cheaper, for there were no copyright laws at this time. As a result, hack writers adapted and translated successful French plays, chief among which were the plays of the prolific Eugène Scribe. Scribe is reported to have written some four hundred plays and pieces for the stage (either alone or in collaboration), of such excellent craftsmanship and to such a successful formula that he was dubbed the inventor of 'the well-made-play' – plays notable mainly for their ingenious twists of plot.

It was common practice throughout the nineteenth century for plays to be pirated, translated, adapted or just used willy-nilly with no regard at all for the playwright. Plays were sold outright to theatrical managements for a fixed sum, and managers made enormous sums of money on popular plays, performed repeatedly, which they had bought for a few pounds. It was not until the copyright laws came into being in the late nineteenth century that playwrights could expect to get substantial payment for their labours.

In 1837 Queen Victoria had ascended the throne. Theatre started to tidy itself up and become more respectable, and one of the reasons for its growing respectability was undoubtedly the interest shown in it by the youthful queen.

The theatre in the second half of the century went through a period of enormous change, matching the equally profound movements going on in economic and social life. Changes occurred in theatre buildings, staging and acting methods, in audiences, in types of play and in attitudes to the theatre. The foundations of modern drama were laid during this period, especially in the last decade of the century. Before discussing some of these issues, however, a word should be said about melodrama, which dominated the entire nineteenth century and gave pleasure to millions.

melodrama

The word itself is derived from the Greek *melos*, meaning song or music, and the French word *drame*, signifying drama. It thus means music drama or, more especially, a drama within which songs are interspersed and in which the action is accompanied by orchestral music. As far as English theatre is concerned, the term was first used to denote a particularly dramatic kind of play performed with music and song throughout. Melodrama grew to prominence as a result of attempts to evade the Theatre Licensing Act of 1737 by presenting legitimate drama in non-patent theatres in such a way that it did not infringe the law. One ingenious solution was to present the play in mime, with essential dialogue written on boards and held up for the audience to read, but a better solution was to introduce songs and accompany the entire action with music. Melodrama of this kind rapidly established itself. The music was almost continuous, with chords breaking up the dialogue or even placed between single words. Quivering strings heightened the emotional tension, for example:

> Ah! what do I see? A man . . ! [*chord*] . . .
> and armed too! [*chord*].
> Perhaps 'tis Wallace. I must be satisfied. [*chord*]

A description of a melodrama performed at Astley's theatre goes into further detail:

111

melodrama

Nearly all the performers had a bar of music to bring them on each time, and another to take them off; a bar when they sat down, and a bar when they got up again; while it took a small overture to get them across the stage. As for the leading lady, every mortal thing she did or said, from remarking that the snow was cold in the first act, to fancying she saw her mother, and then dying, in the last, was preceded by a regular concert.

The first English melodrama seems to have been pirated from the French and presented as *A Tale of Mystery* in 1802. After the 1843 Act, melodrama continued to be performed complete

Artist's impression of a scene from the melodrama *False Shame* by Frank Marshall at the Globe Theatre, 1872. The broad gestures and effects associated with melodrama are very evident.

with music, even though such music was no longer a legal **melodrama** requirement. Gradually, however, the musical element dwindled, leaving the play to be performed as straight drama, but the term 'melodrama' continued to be applied to any play of an extravagant emotional nature, such as the 'heroine-bound-to-the-railroad-track-in-the-path-of-the-oncoming-express' type. Even less sensational plays, but with strong plots, rapid action and clear-cut morality, were referred to as melodrama, such as Irving's great triumph *The Bells.* Perhaps the best-known plays of this kind are *Maria Marten* (or *Murder in the Red Barn*) and *Sweeney Todd, the Demon Barber of Fleet Street.* An eminent critic wrote: 'In melodrama we find that those plays have been most successful that have contained the most prodigious excitement, the most appalling catastrophes, the most harrowing situations – and this without reference to probability of story or consistency of character.' By the end of the century the term 'melodrama' was being used in an uncomplimentary way, much as we would refer today to certain television plays as 'soap opera'.

During the latter half of the nineteenth century London was expanding fast, its population was soaring. (By 1900 it had reached 6½ million, an enormous potential theatre audience.) To encourage more people, especially the middle class, to go to the theatre, managements began to pay more attention to their patrons' comfort and surroundings. Carpets and well-upholstered stall seats were installed, ousting the plain floorboards and benches of the pit. As a result audiences became better behaved; the long bill of fare was shortened and theatre-going became more and more respectable. Royal patronage was conferred and even the Church no longer condemned it – though it did still feel the stage needed purifying. Theatre in its many forms became the main relaxation for the Victorians; it was inexpensive, all tastes were catered for from opera to music hall, classics to melodrama, and there was a growing repertoire of straight plays. It was easy to get to the theatre; cheap, mass forms of public transport linked the provinces to the West End of London. By the 1880s and 1890s all classes attended the theatre and glittering 'first nights' attracted the aristocracy and upper classes. Even at normal performances patrons occupying the stalls, dress circle and boxes were

melodrama expected to wear full evening dress. Matinée performances were introduced in the 1870s, clear evidence of the interest of the leisured classes in theatre-going. In 1895 the seal of respectability was confirmed when the great actor-manager Henry Irving was knighted.

late nineteenth-century theatres

Theatres were becoming elegantly appointed and sumptuously decorated with ornament and gilt plasterwork, floors were carpeted and seating made comfortable. The stage offered greater and greater scenic splendours, many of the major theatres being equipped with impressive hydraulic machinery capable of swiftly raising or lowering whole sections of the stage area. As the stage was now regarded as offering 'a living picture' the fore-stage disappeared, along with any proscenium-arch doors that may have lingered on, and a huge wide gilt frame entirely surrounded the proscenium opening, hence the term 'picture-frame stage'. The first such gilt frame was installed at the Haymarket Theatre in 1881. On-stage, the old-style painted scenery had given way to structured three-dimensional scenery built in high relief complete with real door knobs, real mantelpieces complete with real ornaments, real pictures hanging on the walls, and so on. The old-style wing shutters and backcloths gave place to box sets and free-standing pieces of scenery. By the 1880s the stage was capable of depicting with astonishing realism scenes of liners sinking at sea, racecourses with real galloping horses, train crashes and earthquakes. All this prompted George Bernard Shaw to remark that with the actors and actresses dressed in fashion-plate costumes, productions were '. . . nothing but a tailor's advertisement making sentimental remarks to a milliner's advertisement in the middle of an upholsterer's and decorator's advertisement.' Stage realism was aided by the introduction of electric light in theatres during the late 1880s.

    With the return to more intimate theatres and the 'approach to naturalism' of stage settings came a more easy style of acting. The over-expressive, studied form of acting gave way to a more relaxed, easy style, though the preference for strong curtain lines at the end of scenes in many plays of this period suggests that acting was still some way off naturalism.

late nineteenth-century plays

What of the plays themselves? The bulk of the drama continued to offer relaxation and delight, the kind of entertainment sorely needed by the masses of ill-paid Victorian wage-earners. But as the century reached its end a new seriousness of purpose began to be apparent in the drama – a note of social criticism was struck. As early as the 1860s and following in the steps of Bulwer-Lytton, further examples of plays of social realism were attempted, notably in such examples as Tom Taylor's *Ticket-of-Leave Man,* which looked at the rehabilitation problem of prisoners on release from gaol. T. W. Robertson, in plays like *Society* and *Caste,* demonstrated the chasm existing between social classes. Characterisation became psychologically deeper and social issues were treated frankly. Dialogue, no longer linked exclusively to the servicing of a rapidly moving melodramatic plot, began to acquire a literary flavour as well as a note of social and philosophic enquiry. Notable in this field are Oscar Wilde's, George Bernard Shaw's and Pinero's plays of the 1890s.

The serious play characteristic of this period is the so-called 'problem play' dealing with Victorian dual morality. Men could commit adultery yet still be accepted into polite Victorian society, even though labelled 'fast' or 'philanderers'; but should it be discovered that a married woman had 'committed a serious social indiscretion with a member of the opposite sex' she was banished for ever from society. Yet again play titles bear witness: *A Woman of No Importance, The Notorious Mrs Ebbsmith, Mrs Dane's Defence.* One of the finest of the late nineteenth-century plays of this kind is *The Second Mrs Tanqueray* by Pinero, often regarded as the turning point of English serious drama.

The Second Mrs Tanqueray (1893) was a severe indictment of Victorian social morality. Paula, an attractive and engaging woman 'with a past' has become the second Mrs Tanqueray, married to a fine understanding individual, a pillar of society, who, realising that they will not be accepted into that society (even though *his* credentials are impeccable) takes her to live in the country. But even here her past catches up with her and the couple cannot find the peace of mind to enable them to settle down happily. The play ends in Paula's suicide; Pinero suggesting that Society is to blame. Many plays of this period were not as outspoken. Indeed, in some cases playwrights had to modify their comments and change the endings of their plays, being told by theatre managers that such plays would be found 'unacceptable'.

Newspapers now printed articles on the theatre with extensive reviews of plays, and theatre critics wielded considerable influence, often taking it upon themselves to act as guardians of the public's morals. The bulk of late nineteenth-century drama continued to be of the 'well-made play' type, noted for efficient but contrived plots whose ends were all neatly tied in the final Act. The work of such serious dramatists as there were was aided by William Archer, an enlightened theatre critic, together with others like J. T. Grein who helped found in the 1890s the Independent Theatre and the Stage Society. The aim of both these companies was to give special performances of plays which had a 'literary and artistic rather than a commercial value'. In addition to presenting the plays of Shaw, these societies later gave English premieres of the work of Ibsen, Strindberg, Chekhov, Gorky and Pirandello, who were far ahead of England at this time in terms of serious and 'experimental' drama.

naturalism in European drama

Ibsen in Norway, Strindberg in Sweden, Chekhov in Russia, and other leading European playwrights were writing plays of naturalism and realism. Naturalism in drama was a movement away from the artificial melodrama of the contemporary theatre which bore absolutely no relation to real life. It sought to give on-stage an illusion of the real world through naturalistic plots, dialogue and behaviour, dispensing with highly dramatic but untrue-to-life plots with portraits of villains and heroines and heroes who always won through. Stage dialogue ceased to be epigrammatic or ponderous, plot lines were not neatly tied up at curtain time and characters were believably life-like individuals. Attempts were made to mirror real-life problems and situations, to highlight contemporary issues and to give plays social relevance.

Naturalism then went a step further, leading to realism which tries to create the rock-bottom reality of a situation or incident without actually employing naturalistic methods. The reality of a scene might be conveyed not by using naturalism but by short-cutting it — what mattered was its essence. For instance, in Gorky's play *The Lower Depths*, the reality of the sordid, deadening crush of poverty in the living conditions of the 'down and outs' was sought without resorting to the filthy language and violence undoubtedly inherent in such a way of life. Naturalism aimed at creating an illusion of everyday life — a photographic image; realism went for the reality without necessarily giving a photographic picture.

The pioneer of plays of naturalism and social relevance was Henrik Ibsen (1828–1906). Ibsen spent a lifetime devoted to the theatre; first as a kind of general help in the Norwegian state theatre (his correct title was 'dramaturg') and later as a prolific playwright — he wrote some twenty-three major plays though most were written in exile. The political conduct of Norway he condemned and the Norwegian theatre he considered woefully backward. Essentially Ibsen was a poet, much of his work is written in verse and even his prose has that extra imaginative charge of poetry.

Ibsen began by writing lengthy historical plays (about Norway) which had a modest success in his own country. He then ostensibly deserted the theatre and wrote his two famous non-naturalistic epic verse poems *Brand* and *Peer Gynt*. These were universally recognised as masterpieces and brought him financial security which enabled him to continue living abroad and writing plays. Neither *Brand* nor *Peer Gynt* were expressly written with stage presentation in mind, although both were conceived in stage terms (the theatre at the time was clearly not ready in technical terms to stage them). Ibsen then turned to writing a series of plays in which

naturalism in European drama

naturalism
in
European
drama

he discussed in a naturalistic manner social problems and topics such as the place of women in society and the necessity for truth in public life. Obviously he could not change his style of writing overnight (though he forsook verse and wrote in prose) so that his language is often less than naturalistic and his plots are always meticulously contrived. However, Ibsen's playwriting technique and subject matter were infinitely superior to any other writer of the 1860s, and soon his influence on the theatre began to be felt.

Among his most famous plays of this period are *The Doll's House, Pillars of the Community* and *Hedda Gabler*. In later years he moved away from naturalism towards symbolism (see Chapter 11) with *The Lady From the Sea, The Master Builder* and *When We Dead Awaken*. In such plays, real-life events are given symbolic emphasis suggesting rather more than a simple superficial interpretation might imply. For instance, the character of the strange seaman in *The Lady From the Sea*, whilst appearing as a somewhat strange yet human figure who calls on the lady urging her to return with him to the sea, can be interpreted as an embodiment of the lady's imagination – an element of her sub-conscious – powerful enough to take on a material form and confront and converse with her.

Ibsen was rivalled by the great Swedish writer and experimentalist, August Strindberg (1849–1912). Strindberg passionately believed in a theatre of naturalism and to that end was associated with the Intimate Theatre set up in Stockholm in 1907 which promoted naturalistic drama. His first major play in this mode is the celebrated *Miss Julie* (1888) which has been made into a film as well as into a ballet. In a significant preface to this play he sets out his manifesto of naturalism in theatre. *Miss Julie* is a brilliantly written play with but three main speaking parts. It charts the happenings of a long mid-summer's eve on a large estate in Sweden where the young aristocratic lady of the house succumbs to

Opposite: Vanessa Redgrave in Ibsen's *The Lady From the Sea* at Manchester's 'in-the-round' Royal Exchange Theatre, 1978. Rocks, landing stages and real water covered the entire acting area.

naturalism in European drama

the sexual pre-eminence of a handsome virile manservant — her father's valet. In addition to the battle of the sexes (Strindberg was obsessed with this subject) the play is remarkable for its advanced staging techniques and manner of presentation. Strindberg followed this with other naturalistic plays such as *The Stronger* and then, like Ibsen, went on to write plays of symbolism like *The Dream Play* and *To Damascus*.

Revered in Russia as a short story writer who later developed into a major playwright, Anton Chekhov (1860–1904) is considered an innovator in dramatic form, and his influence on European drama has been immense. Although hailed as a great naturalistic playwright his work, strictly speaking, is not naturalistic at all. It is a very fine cultivation of apparently realistic everyday language, characters and situations, all of which have been carefully assembled to give an illusion of naturalism. What is most powerful about his dialogue are the comments which are implied but never spoken – and his use of significant pauses in the action.

The work of Chekhov, too, veers towards symbolism, as is evident from his first hesitant use of the seagull symbol in his play *The Seagull* and the later more assured handling of symbolism in *The Cherry Orchard*. In this play, the orchard represents different things for each member of the cast and in itself presents a potent symbol of something which once was beautiful and productive but is now only a shadow of its former glory. The term 'Chekhovian drama' implies plays of mood — that of a close-knit family group who are bored, inactive and dull; who recognise their unhappiness and their lack of purpose in life but cannot find the energy to do anything to better their lot. They sink despondently lower and lower under the weight of their largely self-imposed cares, being driven eventually, in certain cases, to suicide. Chekhov's hope was that audiences faced with the pathos of such dreary lives would be alerted to stir themselves out of their own lethargies.

In France, the trend towards naturalism was confirmed by the existence of 'little theatres' — theatres specially created to promote the new drama. The earliest of them, significantly entitled *Le Théâtre Libre* (the Free

Theatre) was under the direction of André Antoine (1858–1943). However, the impetus for drama of greater social relevance came not from theatre people, but from novelists. Writers such as Balzac, Flaubert and the Goncourt brothers, led by Emile Zola (1840–1902), first steered the drama towards 'slice-of-life' theatre. Zola's manifesto of naturalism in the novel and the dramatisation of his own *Thérèse Raquin* paved the way – even though his play was hissed off the stage when first presented. Inevitably after the successes of naturalistic playwrights like Henri Becque and Eugène Brieux a reaction set in, and playwrights increasingly turned to writing works of symbolism.

the arrival of the director

It seems incredible that until the mid-nineteenth century, plays were produced and performed without the need for co-ordination or the guiding hand of a director. However in England during the second half of the century, the require-ment of a particular individual to be responsible for the artistic production of a play became an increasing necessity.

This arose as a direct result of theatre managements paying greater attention to the staging of plays and to audi-ence comfort, now that the middle classes were once again flocking to the theatre. Prior to this there had been very little in the way of organised rehearsals or co-ordinated attention to the staging of plays. The leading actor and actress knew their stuff and acted accordingly without advice from anyone. They were always given centre-stage and supporting actors knew that they had to hover either side of the stars but never them-selves steal the limelight. In addition, most plays were quite unsophisticated and required little or no interpretation; scenery was still nothing more than a pleasant background (however extravagantly conceived) for the action and did not of itself contribute an artistic or symbolic dimension to the play. There was, therefore, little to co-ordinate or direct.

With the movement to tidy up both stage and auditorium, the rise of scenic realism and the arrival of the first plays with a social message, it was apparent that

**the
arrival
of the
director**

co-ordination was becoming necessary. So a special extra person – the overseer – was brought in to direct (a job which previously had been dealt with quite adequately by the stage manager). He was to be responsible for the play's artistic impact; to guide, instruct, coach and generally to ensure that the audience noticed not only the star actors but also the play itself and its message. All aspects of theatrical art – acting, stage design, lighting, costumes and so on – had to contribute to a balanced whole. From being a mere organiser of stage action, the director became the actors' guide, mentor and stimulus and the over-all interpreter of the playwright's script. The profession of director thus became established alongside that of the great late nineteenth-century actor-managers.

Molière in France in the 1660s and 1670s, Garrick in England in the eighteenth century, and Goethe in Germany in the late eighteenth century, had all made some attempts of a directorial nature. However, it is not until the Duke of Saxe-Meiningen in Germany around the 1870s and 1880s undertook with a firm artistic hand the direction of his own troupe of players that it can be said the modern director had arrived. This German nobleman's company became famous throughout Europe (which it toured extensively) for its ensemble work, its meticulous attention to staging details and the naturalistic action of its crowd scenes in which every actor seemed to be an individual. The company became an object lesson to all seriously inclined theatre companies and was widely influential.

The first man to be employed exclusively as a director in England appears to have been Lewis Wingfield, who directed a production of *As You Like It* in 1890 starring Lily Langtree – he was billed as the producer, the name then given to a director.

11

FROM THE EDWARDIANS TO THE ANGRY YOUNG MEN

Attempts at serious drama continued to be somewhat hesitant in the early 1900s, but several dramatists in Britain persisted in their efforts to write and have produced plays which were not simply entertaining but also works of consequence. Among these writers were John Galsworthy, Harley Granville Barker and above all George Bernard Shaw, who commented:

> My reputation has been gained by my persistent struggle to force the public to reconsider its morals. In particular, I regard much current morality as to economic and sexual relations as disastrously wrong; and I regard certain doctrines of the Christian religion as understood in England today with abhorrence. I write plays with the deliberate object of converting the nation to my opinions in these matters.

He went on to do just that!

Galsworthy, whose purpose as novelist and play-wright was to 'throw light on the dark places, the evils and abuses of life, to do so impartially, and for the guidance of others,' had great success with *Justice* (1910). This play attracted the attention of the Home Secretary because it included a scene so harrowing that there was a public outcry. The scene in question took place in gaol, and showed a nervous prisoner forced to endure solitary confinement. As a direct result changes were made in the penal code.

However, the bulk of Britain's theatre-goers flocked to the music halls, the variety theatres, musical comedy and light entertainment. The commercial theatre, solidly supported by the censor, firmly resisted attempts to make straight drama more 'significant', and it was left for smaller, isolated groups to push for less artificial plays.

One such movement took place in the north of England. Throughout the country regional theatre was flourishing with a thriving repertory system – none more energetic than in the north-west, where serious drama was encouraged by a rich benefactress of the arts, Miss Horniman. As a result of her efforts a school of dramatists emerged, known as the Northern School: the two major talents were Harold Brighouse and Stanley Houghton. They wrote plays reflecting contemporary regional life but also asking questions of a more universal nature, such as 'Should the "Fallen woman" always marry the father of her child?' and 'Is it wrong for a girl to seek independence away from home?' These were questions which in the early 1900s parents would have declared capable of only one answer.

Hindle Wakes (1912) by Houghton was a particularly outspoken play and astounded conventional circles. A determined working-class young woman spends a clandestine week-end with the son of a local factory owner. When the affair is accidentally discovered (though no child is involved) she refuses to marry the boy as he is not the sort of man she wants for a husband. She sticks to her guns, even when both sets of parents agree that a marriage is the only honourable solution to what *they* see as a problem. Contemporary moral attitudes were severely flouted in the following passage:

> Boy: But you didn't ever really love me?
> Girl: Love you? Good heavens, of course not! Why on earth should I love you? You were just someone to have a bit of fun with. You were an amusement – a lark.

Boy: Fanny. Is that all you cared for me?
Girl: How much did you care for me?
Boy: But it's not the same . . . I'm a man . . .
Girl: You're a man, and I was your little fancy. Well,
I'm a woman, and YOU were MY little fancy.
You wouldn't prevent a woman enjoying herself
as well as a man, if she takes it into her head?

The freedom with which such matters were now discussed on-stage reflected changing moral attitudes, especially those of the young. There remained, however, very many topics which were taboo, together with expressions which the censor would not permit; none the less the climate was becoming far more receptive to a drama of enquiry.

At the Royal Court Theatre, London, and later at the Savoy Theatre, avant-garde productions of Shakespeare, Maeterlinck – a Belgian poet and dramatist and one of the best known symbolist playwrights – and W. B. Yeats were presented by the Barker-Vedrenne management (with Harley Granville-Barker as director), whose production approach nudged symbolism and expressionism. Symbolism in drama came as a direct result of the move away from naturalism in the 1890s It is 'poetic' drama as opposed to prose drama, and attempts to express via symbols a more complex reaction than that conveyed by simple stage illusion. The settings of symbolist plays are intentionally unreal, the dialogue and characters non-naturalistic, the action metaphysical. It has been described as 'the abandonment of the appearance of life in favour of its spirit, symbolically represented'.

The First World War temporarily halted such movements but gave a boost to musicals and light entertainment. *Chu-Chin-Chow* ran for 2238 consecutive performances. Revue was introduced and became synonymous with the name of C. B. Cochran, the leading impresario of the day. Cinema, by now well established, sealed the death of the great stage melodramatic spectaculars

In the 1920s intellectual drama re-emerged and was found on the fringe of the West End commercial theatre. Little new native drama was written, but there were enthusiastic revivals of Greek tragedy, Chekhov and Restoration and

Elizabethan drama. Expressionism, a short-lived movement in drama in the 1920s, stood in direct opposition to the naturalistic theatre. It attempted to create on-stage, especially in stage design, the inner psychological struggles of characters. Typically such plays presented the conflict of the 'little man' and the uncaring, insensitive world at large, or his struggles against huge, machine-like corporations.

The gay twenties delighted in brittle, light comedy, and heralded the arrival of the American musical – in the shape of *No, No, Nanette*. Noël Coward burst on to the theatrical scene and was instantly hailed as the spokesman of the younger generation. Some of his plays, such as *Fallen Angels*, were considered immoral, but *Hay Fever* (1925) showed his real talent as a writer of elegant high comedy.

Side by side with the professional theatre came the rapid development in the early 1900s of the amateur theatre movement. During the Edwardian era amateur theatre became established on a nationwide footing, resulting in the formation of the British Drama League in 1919. Theatre had become a truly popular art form; acting groups and theatre societies proliferated and amateur drama festivals created a healthy rivalry. On the professional side acting schools and drama academies were established to promote dramatic art and to provide vocational training. This was the time when, in spite of Noël Coward's quips, it was now acceptable and possible to 'put one's daughter on the stage'.

The drama of the inter-war years and up to 1956 was one of comforting assurance. It seldom questioned any serious social issue and hardly ever strayed outside the confines of middle-class drawing-rooms. Plays had a beginning, a middle and an end, in which no one ever uttered a four-letter word, and everyone usually dressed for dinner. They were pleasurable interludes enabling Aunt Edna to while away a couple of hours at the theatre without having to trouble her head over too-serious matters. Although immensely talented and professional, the playwrights of this period were writing for an unthinking, happy-go-lucky society, shortly to be swept away by world events. Playwrights concerned themselves with either metaphysical speculation on subjects far removed from the everyday world – for instance J. B. Priestley discussing the

The deliciously infamous *ménage à trois* in Noël Coward's *Design for Living* – the brilliant Greenwich Theatre revival which came into the West End in 1982. (Maria Aitken, Ian Ogilvy and Gary Bond.)

phenomenon of time, James Bridie on the nature of the Devil, and T. S. Eliot on the concept of guilt − or they wrote plays about contemporary, comfortable middle-class life in which characters burst through the French windows from the garden enquiring: 'Who's for tennis?' The work of women dramatists, including Dodie Smith, Gordon Daviot (a pseudonym), Esther McCracken and Margaret Kennedy, featured among a large number of popular light plays.

With the economic collapse in 1929, theatre responded with a mild attack of patriotism − Noël Coward's *Cavalcade* in 1931 was enormously successful − but light entertainment continued to dominate. One major exception − a play which clearly reflected contemporary problems − was *Love on the Dole*, produced in 1934. Adapted from Walter Greenwood's novel, it had to be nursed into success but eventually transferred from Manchester to London, where the *Daily Telegraph* described it as: '. . . the play closest to the life of the times . . . reflecting the social evils of the age and combining a sincerity of purpose with a sense of humour and a regard for character.' The play which launched the actress Wendy Hiller on her brilliant career, it depicted unemployment in the north and secured the distinction of being mentioned in a parliamentary debate on the subject.

During the years of the Second World War, London's theatres were officially closed. However, long before the end of hostilities many had re-opened, and with the end of the flying bomb menace in 1944 some forty major London theatres were again in business.

Of war plays during these decades there was a notable absence. *Journey's End* by R. C. Sheriff (recently very successfully revived) was a First World War play which appeared in 1928: it gave a compassionate and harrowing account of life in the trenches. Its Second World War counterpart was *Flarepath* (1942) by Terence Rattigan, dealing with the stresses and strains of RAF aircrews and their women in wartime. However, the times did not lend themselves to frank discussion of such acute realism.

There was a great interest in this period in the thriller play, not only from the pen of the queen of whodunits herself, Agatha Christie (*The Mousetrap*, which opened in 1952, is still running), but also from such playwrights as Barré Lyndon, whose play *The Amazing Dr Clitterhouse* opened in New York in 1936 and was frequently and successfully revived in the 1940s. Emlyn Williams contributed *A Murder Has Been Arranged* (1930) and *Night Must Fall* (1935), and James Bridie, the Scottish playwright, began his career in the theatre with *The Anatomist,* the story of the surgeon Dr Knox and his collection of corpses provided by the grave robbers and murderers Burke and Hare. Bridie continued with further eerie plays of good and evil, notably *Mr Bolfrey* (1943), in which the Devil materialises in a Scottish manse as a local cleric, and *Dr Angelus,* a Victorian-type murder play set in contemporary times. Bridie's contribution to the drama of the 1930s–1950s is immense – he wrote some thirty-four full-length plays, not all of them so ghoulish as those mentioned above, though most of them are remote from the everyday world. In 1949 he gave Edith Evans one of her very best parts as the unhappy Lady Pitts, full of drink and chatter, in *Daphne Laureola.*

J. B. Priestley also had numerous successes with comedies, dramas and plays which on the surface appeared realistic enough but which eventually suggested there were more things in heaven and earth than are generally dreamt of. Indeed some of them, like *Johnson over Jordan* (1939) and *They Came to a City* (1943), began with situations in which the characters had just died, and dealt with life after death.

In the late 1940s distinguished revivals of the classics were produced by the Old Vic Company at the New Theatre, featuring the work of the reigning trio of English actors, Laurence Olivier, Ralph Richardson and John Gielgud. All were subsequently knighted for services to the stage.

Verse plays too had an intense but short-lived vogue in the 1940s and 1950s. Christopher Fry made his mark with such plays as *The Lady's Not for Burning* and *The Dark Is Light Enough,* romantic plays of dazzling verbal cascades. The cast of the former included the young Richard Burton.

Most of the successful inter-war playwrights had prolific outputs, the most consistently popular being Terence Rattigan. Beginning with *French Without Tears* (1936), his box office hits include several which are still occasionally revived today – *The Winslow Boy* (1946), the story of the celebrated trial of a naval cadet expelled for stealing; *The Browning Version* (1948), in which the emotional relationships between a dedicated schoolmaster, his pupils and his wife are revealingly explored; and *The Deep Blue Sea* (1952), an unusual piece about a doomed love affair between an ex-RAF pilot and the middle-aged wife of an established lawyer. He is also remembered for the highly successful *Separate Tables* (1954) and *Ross* (1960), the former sympathetically exposing the loneliness and heartache among the clientele of a provincial private hotel, and the latter recounting episodes in the life of Lawrence of Arabia.

Less successful – his hits as a playwright tended to be erratic – is Peter Ustinov, who received much applause in the 1950s for *The Love of Four Colonels* and *Romanoff and Juliet*. Since then he has had a few further successes but his plays have not generally been as well received as his stage, film, television and after-dinner appearances.

Critics have tended to label the plays of the 1940s and 1950s minor and parochial, but they were eminently commercial plays written for the audiences of the day and seldom aspired to be anything more. Only the plays of Graham Greene, the celebrated novelist who turned his attention to playwriting when in his fifties, are of greater significance, though they do not match his novels. *The Living Room* (1953), *The Potting Shed* (1957) and *The Complaisant Lover* (1959) all had a serious tone and were successful at the box office, though it is interesting that today his plays are not revived, unlike those of Rattigan, Priestley and Emlyn Williams.

Then in 1955 and 1956 two revolutionary productions were seen in London which contrasted sharply with anything that had gone before; as a result, the course of the somewhat complacent English theatre was violently altered. The first was Samuel Beckett's *Waiting for Godot*, surely the most significant play of the century to date, with its baffling picture of two tramps on an almost deserted stage waiting for a character called Godot who never arrives. The second turning-point was John Osborne's *Look Back in Anger*, which gave the language a new expression for contemporary youth, 'angry young man'.

the United States of America

There was no distinct national drama in the USA until after the First World War. Until that time, American theatres were full of British and Continental imports. It was the practice of the day for the English actor-managers to tour America with their European successes. The first US playwright who began to make his mark with American characters and American social themes was Bronson Howard. He was followed by William Clyde Fitch, George Kelly and Maxwell Anderson. The most celebrated of the early US playwrights was Eugene O'Neill, winner of the Nobel Prize for Literature in 1936, and the Pulitzer Prize. But once established, the American theatre became a powerful force and American plays and playwrights became as familiar in England as English ones in America.

Eugene O'Neill (1888–1953) had a prolific output of some twenty or more major plays as well as one-acters. His range of work is extremely broad, from the neo-classical trilogy of *Mourning Becomes Electra,* which he set in the American Civil War, based on Aeschylus' *Oresteia,* to *Long Day's Journey Into Night* staged in 1956 after his death.

Between 1940 and the mid-1950s American theatre dominated the English-speaking world. Until Osborne's *Look Back In Anger* in 1956, American playwrights, acting methods, direction and stage design were familiar to and overshadowed the English theatre. After O'Neill came Elmer Rice, the pioneer of expressionist drama in America; Thornton Wilder, another anti-naturalistic playwright who wrote the well-known *Our Town* and two earlier plays on which the musical *Hello Dolly* was based; Lillian Hellman, America's first successful woman playwright; Clifford Odets and perhaps the most famous trio of US playwrights, Tennessee Williams (1914–83), Arthur Miller (b. 1915) and Edward Albee (b. 1928). Pre-eminent in comedy and farce is George S. Kaufman who wrote *The Man Who Came To Dinner.*

The plays of Tennessee Williams are exotic – even by American standards – containing social outcasts, homosexuals, nymphomaniacs, cowards, bullies and larger-than-life characters. Although sensational in every sense of the word his plays are among the key works of modern drama –

the
United
States of
America

The Glass Menagerie (1945), *A Streetcar Named Desire* (1947), *Summer and Smoke* (1947) and *Cat on a Hot Tin Roof* (1955) – and many have been turned into excellent films. Most people will recall the film of *A Streetcar Named Desire* which teamed the unlikely pair of Marlon Brando and Vivien Leigh. Set in sleazy downtown New Orleans, the play explores with shocking honesty yet with consummate skill, the psycho-sexual world of conflict and suffering; Blanche Dubois, a fragile and fading 'southern belle', retreats into a twilight world of self-fantasy only to have her make-believe world violently shattered by the husband of her sister (with whom she has taken refuge), an insensitive brutal tough who so harasses her that he eventually drives her permanently into her twilight world. Williams is fond of exploring the stress of psychological disorders and *A Streetcar Named Desire* is a masterpiece of harrowing theatre. But he could be tender, too – as in *The Glass Menagerie* and *Summer and Smoke,* both of which detail the unsuccessful love affairs of lonely, sensitive women.

The lurid sunsets of Williams' plays contrast with the hard reality of Arthur Miller's work. Williams concerns himself mainly with women, Miller with men; both deal in psychological realism. Miller's plays are regularly in today's theatre repertoire; several have already achieved the status of classics. Among his plays are *All My Sons, Death of a Salesman, The Price* and *The Crucible. Death of a Salesman* (1949) has received the most acclaim and has been called a modern tragedy – a story of failure, an American dream that dissolved. Shortly after the play opened Miller wrote an important essay entitled *Tragedy and the Common Man* pointing out that portentous tragedy was not solely the prerogative of kings and princes – it could happen to the man next door, and be every bit as terrible. In the play, Willy Loman, the salesman of the title, is a small man in every sense of the word. Unsuccessful and ageing, he is losing contact with reality in a highly competitive world, facing unemployment and financial ruin. Caught out over a shady affair with another woman, he crumbles under his troubles and commits suicide by crashing his car, the insurance money securing his family's future. America worships a success story; here was the reverse, raising questions of inadequacy – the fault of the little man or of society at large? The play is a powerful and disturbing piece of theatre.

Psychological stress is also the theme in many of Edward Albee's plays. He has never quite managed to repeat the enormous success of his early works *Zoo Story* (1958) and *Who's Afraid of Virginia Woolf?* (1961), but such plays as *Tiny Alice* and *A Delicate Balance* are fine pieces of theatrical writing concerning isolation and despair in an unsettled world.

the influence of the director

Just before the First World War new trends emerged with regard to staging, reflecting the work of such designers as Edward Gordon Craig and Adolphe Appia. Craig pioneered many developments in stage design and advocated a theatre of non-realistic decor and atmospheric lighting, in which the visual impact was of paramount importance and the director was a dictator. Adolphe Appia, a Swiss, worked along similar lines. The principle behind his work was that of total theatre; he advocated a theatre of atmosphere rather than naturalism. Both Craig and Appia as designers, with their understanding of the importance of total theatre and that of a master mind controlling it, considerably influenced the directors who followed.

The Russian influence on European drama in the field of stage design and direction has been considerable. The model of all modern European directors is Konstantin Stanislavsky (1863–1938), the Russian actor, teacher and director, and co-founder of the Moscow Art Theatre (MAT). Stanislavsky was among the first to explore systematically the art of staging plays and although his work was heavily based on the actor's contribution (he founded the influential Stanislavsky system), he was fascinated by all aspects of the theatre. He moved away from the blatant theatricality of the contemporary stage, insisting on naturalistic costumes and settings with an acting style to match, which was far less histrionic and declamatory than that currently employed. Several of his productions are still in the repertoire of the MAT. He wrote a number of books on the theatre, especially on acting: *An*

Stage design by Adolphe Appia, 1924, for 'a wild rocky place' in *Die Walküre*. The different acting levels and varying light and shade are Appia's hallmarks.

Actor Prepares, Building a Character and *Stanislavsky Rehearses Othello*, which have become standard texts on the subjects.

Stanislavsky's work in Russia was carried on by Vsevolod Meyerhold (1874–1943), another actor, director and theorist who worked for a time with Stanislavsky at the MAT before setting up his own company and working for the new Soviet government at his Theatre of Meyerhold. He developed a system of acting known as 'bio-mechanics' which regarded the actor almost as a physical machine, capable of considerable mimetic and acrobatic effectiveness. His actors were trained almost exclusively in physical agility, especially in the circus arts of tumbling, acrobatic and gymnastic techniques. He also invented 'constructivism' in staging – employing totally non-naturalistic sets constructed from wood, metal and machinery. A tree might be a mass of iron pipes; a mountain slope made of corrugated steel. He is remembered for his productions of the plays of the Russian dramatist Mayakovsky and for the now-famous production of Gogol's play *The Government Inspector* in which, in the last Act, actors were replaced by dummies.

Yevgeny Vakhtangov (1883–1922) was another renowned Soviet director and one-time pupil of Stanislavsky. Around the time of the Revolution he began experimenting in acting and production techniques and broke away from MAT to set up the Moscow Dramatic Studio, later known as the Third Workshop. His style of direction was akin to most of the leading avant-garde directors – non-naturalistic, leaning towards expressionism – but he continued to recognise the contribution of the individual actor.

As German drama moved sharply away from naturalism in the first decades of the twentieth century it took most of avant-garde European drama with it. The new drama dismissed all attempts at illusionistic theatre and created new staging techniques involving the atmospheric use of lighting, little scenery and a great deal of mechanical-type staging – Toller's *The Machine Wreckers* (1922) is a typical example. Not surprisingly the director again came to the fore with such eminent and influential practitioners as Max Reinhardt, Erwin Piscator and Bertolt Brecht.

Max Reinhardt (1873–1943) was the first director to acquire an international reputation. He is best known for his handling of huge spectacular productions in large non-theatre spaces, such as *Oedipus Rex* in the Schumann Circus in Vienna, *Everyman* in the cathedral square in Salzburg, and *The Miracle* at Olympia, London. His specialities were visual splendour, stunning crowd pictures and effective lighting, but he was also responsible for many intimate and successful small-stage productions in Berlin and elsewhere.

Erwin Piscator (1893–1966) was a follower of Reinhardt's methods. He too favoured productions on a grand scale but he liked to raise social and political issues. He coined the term 'epic theatre' — theatre which draws the audience's attention to the social and political content of plays. He did this by doing away with the theatre of illusion, substituting a theatre which did not suggest reality; dramatic suspense was not relied on and identification with characters not encouraged, with the result that the play unfolded through a series of short non-consecutive scenes. Devices such as song, masks, filmed passages, direct audience address, slogans and non-naturalistic settings were used. In this respect Piscator's approach is similar to that of Brecht.

The Nazis soon appreciated the value of theatre in propaganda terms and developed it accordingly. They recognised the enormous power of ritual and spectacle and sponsored open-air productions on a grand scale. Such theatre is reflected in the Nazi rallies which Hitler engineered. Confronted with the rise of Nazism, Reinhardt, Piscator and Bertolt Brecht, the most influential of the contemporary German playwrights and directors, fled from Germany to work in America and elsewhere.

Two notable directors in Britain were Michael Saint-Denis and Tyrone Guthrie, both of whom worked at the Old Vic Theatre in London. Although born a Frenchman, Saint-Denis (1897–1971) had considerable influence on the English stage and on the training of many of our eminent actors. From 1946–52 he was the general director of the Old Vic Theatre School as well as being responsible for a number of splendid productions; he became a director of the theatre itself in 1950 for a couple of years, and directed *Oedipus Rex, A Month in the Country* and *Electra*.

Working alongside Saint-Denis was Tyrone Guthrie (1900–71), who was also a director at the Old Vic, on and off, for a number of years. Guthrie has been described as 'restless, experimental, unorthodox, brilliant and a huge influence on the shape and style of modern theatres'. He pioneered the concept of the open stage and was largely responsible for the open stages at the Shakespeare Festival Theatre at Stratford in Canada, the Nottingham Playhouse, the Crucible at Sheffield, and the Chichester Festival Theatre.

Guthrie was also eminent in the field of directing

Shakespeare, notching up several very famous and some
infamous productions. A production of *Henry VIII* was
considered 'notoriously eccentric' by some critics, though his
All's Well That Ends Well in which the army scenes were set
as though the cast were the original 1939–45 North African
'Desert Rats' was better received, as was a production of
Troilus and Cressida with Wendy Hiller playing Helen of Troy
as a 'floosie' of the gay 1920s. Pursuing his ideas of open
staging Guthrie directed a much acclaimed production of a
medieval Scottish play, *Ane Pleasant Satyre of the Thrie
Estaitis* in Edinburgh in 1948. He directed for the Royal
Shakespeare Company and worked in Canada and in
America, where a theatre in Minneapolis is named after him.

**the
influence
of the
director**

12

THEATRE
TODAY

Look Back in Anger

In 1956 the drama reflected in one particular play and in the feelings of one particular young man the culmination of a mood – the mood of the post-war years. After the Second World War and after a decade of readjustment to peace, the brave new world so long promised was failing to materialise. The post-war generation, used to greater freedom of expression than their parents in terms of clothes, lifestyle and opinions, were becoming disillusioned, critical and outspoken. Largely rejecting the Church, the bonds of matrimony and conventional behaviour, the young (and by now the not-so-young) were cultivating a growing social and political consciousness. The invasion of Hungary and the events of Suez, both in 1956, were additional proof that all was not right with the world.

The voice of youthful discontent was echoed in the novels of Kingsley Amis and John Wain, and in theatrical terms by John Osborne in his play *Look Back in Anger* in the person of Jimmy Porter, its lead character. Subsequently, critics designated this play as the fuse which fired the succeeding 'revolution' in the theatre. Jimmy Porter, a graduate of a redbrick university, loudly criticised almost everybody and everything around him. He trumpeted throughout the play his manifold dissatisfaction with the state of his world and the world at large; to the audience he seemed to sound the right notes.

Although the form of the play was traditional, its tone was new. It was abrasive, outspoken and forceful. It scarcely seemed to matter to audiences that Jimmy Porter was himself undisciplined, insecure and lazy, or that the targets which he attacked so vociferously were multiple and his arguments unfocused. Neither did it seem to matter that Jimmy, in order to earn a living, aspired no higher than keeping a sweet stall in the local market. The tone of the play demanded attention;

The original cast of Osborne's *Look Back in Anger* at the Royal Court Theatre, May 1956. Mary Ure (Alison), Alan Bates (Cliff), Helena Hughes (Helena) and Kenneth Haigh (Jimmy Porter).

something was being said in a compelling manner. Other budding playwrights were quick to respond and echo Osborne's example in plays which were a far cry from the genteel kind of drama previously purveyed on the West End stage.

The new work was actively encouraged by the English Stage Company whose policy was to discover and foster new playwriting talent, which they did very successfully with such names as Ann Jellicoe, N. F. Simpson, John Arden and Arnold Wesker. They presented at the Royal Court on Sunday evenings new plays in productions 'without decor', and under club theatre conditions, for many of the new plays would never have been licensed by the Lord Chamberlain for public presentation.

Waiting for Godot

Nineteen fifty-six was also the year in which another significant play appeared in London's West End — *Waiting for Godot* by Samuel Beckett. The play is in two parts and described as a tragi-comedy. It has no plot and only two main characters, who appear to be tramps; the cast is completed by two other men and a boy. The action, if such it can be called, takes place on an almost empty stage. Then and now interpretations are many and varied, but it was labelled 'Theatre of the Absurd', a form of avant-garde theatre mainly indulged in by European playwrights in the 1950s. ('Absurd' was interpreted as 'out of harmony'; such plays discussed in a metaphysical way the absurdity of the human condition.) Plays of this kind obviously could not be interpreted literally, but clearly had significance if the key could be found. *Waiting for Godot* was one of the earliest modern plays to reduce scenery, lighting changes, action and plot to a minimum. Act 1 simply calls for 'A country road. A tree. A low mound. Evening'; Act 2, 'Next day, same time, same place. The tree has four or five leaves.' The play's text indicates that the description 'tree' and 'country road' need not be interpreted too naturalistically. Although there is considerable stage business with personal properties such as

The play that shattered contemporary theatrical conventions –
Beckett's *Waiting for Godot,* in Peter Hall's 1955 production at The
Arts Theatre. (Peter Woodthorpe, Paul Daneman as the 'tramps',
Peter Bull as Pozzo.)

boots, hats, rope and bags, the play is punctuated with
silences and a sense of waiting. There is no forward action.
There is no story line. The play ends inconclusively. Yet the
text provides many visual and aural images, and in spite of
one extended speech of seeming nonsense, language is skilfully used even though the efficiency of language as such is
questioned. Here indeed was another play with a difference.

Look Back in Anger and *Waiting for Godot* suggested
a radical reappraisal and a new approach to the content and
expression of a play's text. The productions described below
suggested in addition a new method of acting and presentation

**Brecht
and
alienation**

Brecht and alienation

Also in 1956 the Berliner Ensemble, a leading theatre company from East Berlin, visited London. They presented a programme of plays which included *The Caucasian Chalk Circle* and *Mother Courage* by Bertolt Brecht (1898–1956), the Company's founder and artistic director. His influence on theatre has been immense both as a playwright and as a director, especially in his approach to staging. Awareness of his work had earlier been widespread but here was an opportunity to see it in action, and it proved stimulating. Above all, such Brechtian productions demonstrated that a fully equipped traditional proscenium-arch theatre was no longer needed –

A scene from Brecht's *The Days of the Commune* first produced in Germany at the Karl Marx Stadt civic theatre in 1956. Note the Brechtian staging.

plays could be effectively staged in any open space. It was a
new approach to theatre and undoubtedly influenced many
young contemporary playwrights and directors.

Brecht, a Marxist, wanted theatre to be a more
objective experience for his audience, and to this end
employed methods in his writing and production approach
which constantly reminded the audience that they should not
get emotionally involved but think about the meaning of the
play. He attempted to de-mystify theatre – actors were seen
as such, stage-hands were visible, scenery was strictly
functional, stage lighting and equipment were not concealed,
and scene changes took place in full view of the audience.
The play itself did not unroll in a leisurely, narrative fashion
but consisted of a series of short, self-contained episodes;
furthermore the action was broken up with songs 'to enable
the audience to reflect' on what they had seen. Actors were
encouraged not to immerse themselves in the roles they
played but to adopt an acting style which was illustrative
rather than illusionistic – like an onlooker recounting to a
passer-by the events of a street accident. And because
suspense often prompts an audience to wonder 'Then what
happened?' rather than 'Why did this happen?', Brecht
informed them of the outcome of a scene in advance, by
means of placards, filmed projections or a singing story-teller.

All of this adds up to Brecht's technique and style
which he called *Verfremdungseffekt*. Often translated as
'alienation effect', it is perhaps better appreciated as
'estrangement'. It is a deliberate, politically motivated method
of distancing the audience to encourage them to take a stand
on social issues. Ionesco, a Rumanian playwright of the 1950s,
described Brecht as a postman because he was always
delivering messages! However, in Brecht's favour it must
be said that many of the images in his plays are so striking,
the songs are so enjoyable (who has not heard of 'Mack
the Knife'?) and the over-all result so theatrically effective
that, paradoxically (and despite Brecht's technique), it is possible to enjoy the plays on a theatrical level alone. The term
'Brechtian' has now entered theatre vocabulary to indicate
this epic or narrative style of writing and production, even
when detached from any political message.

Joan Littlewood and Theatre Workshop

One of the most significant theatre practitioners of the 1950s and 1960s was Joan Littlewood (b. 1914). Both founder of a theatre company and a director of note, she was also the first person in England to lead a genuine ensemble drama group. She founded Theatre Workshop in 1945 which toured one-night stands mainly in the north of England before settling into its permanent home in 1953 in the Theatre Royal, Stratford East, a working-class district of London. Here Littlewood directed a number of highly successful plays, many of them classics, and had several modern plays transfer to the West End. She established her own particular kind of direction, believing in the co-operative form of theatrical production in which everybody – actors, even stage-hands, as well as the director – was encouraged to contribute to its development. She preferred to work from a scenario (not a finished text) on which the company could get to work with improvisation and suggestion.

Littlewood was also instrumental in helping new writers to get their plays performed and positively enjoyed working on scripts which were only ideas or incomplete; in this way she staged works by Brendan Behan and Shelagh Delaney. In that seminal year of 1956 Littlewood produced Behan's play *The Quare Fellow.* She thrived on theatre with a political tinge and also musicals – several of her productions continue to be revived today, notably *Oh What a Lovely War,* first performed in 1963, a devastating satire on the carnage and destruction of the First World War. *Fings Ain't Wot They Used T' Be* (1959), another musical, transferred to the West End and ran for 897 performances at the Garrick Theatre. Littlewood had a conception of theatre for the masses, a truly popular theatre which would be fun; unhappily her 'fun palaces' were never realised, but her methods of play production have many followers.

kitchen sink drama

Realistic working-class drama came to the fore in the 1950s with such plays as Shelagh Delaney's *A Taste of Honey*

(1958), Arnold Wesker's early plays, especially *Roots* (1959) and *The Kitchen* (1958–61), John Arden's *Live Like Pigs* (1958) and Edward Bond's *Saved* (1965), which were given the popular collective term 'kitchen sink drama'. The expression implied that the action, as John Russell Taylor points out, 'revolved physically or psychologically around the kitchen sink'. Previously it had been the drawing-room. But there was no clearly defined kitchen sink drama movement as such – it was a term much loved by the popular press highlighting the more obvious differences between established playwrights and the 'new wave' dramatists of the late 1950s and 1960s.

One feature of the new dramatists, however, was inescapable – most of them came from working-class backgrounds and very few had attended university. Practically all of them were under forty and many under thirty. Some had been actors – for instance John Osborne, Harold Pinter, Henry Livings and Alan Ayckbourn. The theatre, which had for so long been the preserve of the middle-class playwright writing for a middle-class audience, was now injected with a youthful, no-nonsense approach. As a result, what theatre offered changed rapidly from plays of comforting assurance to dramas of acid outspokenness. It reflected some of the difficulties of the younger generation in a world of staggering problems and inadequate solutions, conditions which had bred widespread social alienation.

A glance at two plays of Shelagh Delaney, from industrial Lancashire, will confirm the point. *A Taste of Honey* (1958) is set in a slum and charts the wayward course of a teenage schoolgirl and her tarty mother. There is no father around, and the girl, left to fend for herself, has casual relations with a couple of men and is made pregnant by a negro sailor. Deserted by the sailor and her mother (who has gone off with her latest man) she is befriended by a gentle homosexual art student who cares for her until the mother returns – once more alone – when he leaves. It is a somewhat squalid tale made even more so by the passive acceptance, by both mother and daughter, of their situation. The second play, *The Lion in Love* (1960), again focuses on a mother and daughter relationship but this time the emphasis is on the

**kitchen
sink
drama**

middle-aged, drink-sodden mother and embittered father, locked in a loveless marriage from which neither can escape.

Up to the early 1960s theatre was still considered primarily a literary medium but by the mid-decade this had changed. With the notable exception of such playwrights as John Mortimer, Robert Bolt, Joe Orton and Tom Stoppard, the literary element was being superseded by dialogue and situations of an overt realism, while language and vocal effects were vying with physical and visual effects. Edward Bond, for instance, became especially noted for the violence of his images. Enchantment, charm and literacy were quitting the stage; harsh reality was taking over. Amid a general air, as Ronald Hayman puts it, of 'modish hostility to style, literature and sophistication', the drama was becoming abrasive. It was apparent that the well-born, well-educated, well-spoken heroes of the plays of Noël Coward and Terence Rattigan were giving way to the anti-heroes of a working-class drama. With cast lists set lower in the social scale, the social graces, particularly with respect to language and conversation, were lower too.

theatre of cruelty

In 1964 a systematic exploration of styles of acting and presentation was undertaken by the directors Charles Marowitz and Peter Brook with members of the Royal Shakespeare Company. It took place in London in open workshop sessions under the general title of Theatre of Cruelty. The title derives from the French actor, Antonin Artaud (1896–1948) and his theories on a revolutionary new form of theatre. These sessions involved improvisation as well as effects calculated to shock audiences, such as nudity (at that time unknown in serious theatre), screaming, and the miming of 'unspeakable actions'. Peter Brook's production of *The Persecution and Assassination of Marat as Performed by the Inmates of the Asylum of Charenton under the Direction of the Marquis de Sade* by the German Peter Weiss was presented by the RSC and starred Glenda Jackson – in a famous scene whipping with her long hair the naked torso of de Sade. The play, still often revived by student groups, is affectionately known as the *Marat-Sade*.

Theatre of Cruelty workshops, the effect of American alternative theatre groups and Method acting – a serious but controversial approach to acting taught at the Actors' Studio in New York – had a profound effect on the burgeoning fringe theatre in Britain. The fringe also benefited enormously from the abolition of stage censorship in 1968.

the end of stage censorship

In the 1950s and early 1960s times were changing and the Lord Chamberlain was forced to recognise the fact. The censorship issue was brought to a head in 1965 when two plays, John Osborne's *A Patriot for Me* and Edward Bond's *Saved,* were denied a licence for public presentation unless massively cut. The English Stage Company, who wished to present them at the Royal Court Theatre, refused to emasculate the plays and subsequently presented them for club members only – the only way of evading the law of stage censorship. *A Patriot for Me* is based on the true story of an intelligence officer blackmailed for his homosexual activities. The play won the *Evening Standard* prize for the best play of 1965 but the Lord Chamberlain refused it a public licence on the grounds that (among other things) there were scenes in the play in which 'men embrace each other and are seen in bed together'. The more controversial *Saved* contained a scene in which a baby was stoned to death by a gang of psychopathically violent youths. It also included a number of four-letter words and further scenes of a sexually provocative nature to which the Lord Chamberlain objected. Strong feelings were aroused by both plays, which eventually led to a debate in the House of Commons and the ending of censorship.

In 1968 the Theatres Act was passed, abolishing stage censorship. In effect, censorship passed from the Lord Chamberlain to the public. If a member of the public thinks that a play is 'obscene' and 'liable to deprave and corrupt' he or she can lodge a formal complaint with the Director of Public Prosecutions. The result of the Act was that drama was given much greater freedom and, contrary to all expectation, did not result overnight in a theatre of sensational licentiousness!

the influence of American alternative theatre

American influence on fringe theatre in Britain has been considerable, through the work of off-Broadway troupes and also indirectly through Method acting, a system of acting taught at the Actors' Studio in New York, founded by Lee Strasberg in 1948. It gained prominence in the 1960s when the Studio began producing plays on Broadway. The Method places considerable emphasis on improvisation and the ability of the actor to immerse himself in his role, and is especially suited to modern drama where the accent is on realism. Its fostering of improvisation techniques endeared itself immediately to fringe groups.

The rise of fringe theatre in the United States evolved (as it did in Britain) as a revolt against the complacent middle-class theatre of the 1950s and as a reaction against the values of contemporary society. The movement in the States was considerably helped by the presence on most university campuses of theatres and departments which studied theatre arts. America too was unhampered by the British system of censorship. In America managements were restrained only by what they knew they could get away with without being prosecuted.

The American influence was physically brought to Britain by the visits to London in 1961 and to Edinburgh in 1967 of the Living Theatre group and La Mama respectively. Many alternative theatre groups such as these worked and *lived* as communities when they first emerged, their members having dropped out of established educational institutes or employment. (The Living Theatre, which has now existed for some thirty years, literally grew up with its members.) One thing which set these groups apart was that they were not primarily concerned with entertainment as a product to be sold. They were far more interested in the message or exploration of the operation of theatre rather than performance. They performed in non-traditional acting spaces and deliberately attempted to break down the separation between actor and audience. The actors of the Living Theatre provoked their audiences into participation, arguing, insulting and haranguing them in order to break down the typical reserve and impassive nature of conventional theatre audiences. Acting was from that time no longer seen as something coolly, stylishly and lyrically performed in a space isolated from its audience by a proscenium arch or other invisible barrier. The action which invaded the audience was strident and forceful and demanded response. It dealt with widely felt contemporary issues and not just the problems of an elitist society.

American writers are still influencing British fringe theatre. The most promising younger American writers today are Sam Shepard (b. 1943) and David Mamet (b. 1947). Shepard is from Off-Off-Broadway (the American fringe) and his work is very avant-garde; it is vital, forceful and fundamental. Among his plays are *Tooth of Crime*, which has a rock 'n' roll star as its leading character, and *Buried Child*, which won the Pulitzer Prize in 1979. Mamet has recently been writing for the cinema (*The Postman Always Rings Twice*) but his earlier work included *Sexual Perversity in Chicago* (1974) and *A Life in the Theatre* (1978).

fringe theatre in Britain

Charles Marowitz and Jim Haynes, both Americans, are regarded as having been in the forefront of presenting 'alternative' or 'fringe' theatre in Britain. Haynes began in Edinburgh where he acquired premises (a disused brothel) for the original Traverse Theatre Club in 1963, in which he presented the best of the avant-garde American and European playwrights of the time.

Fringe theatre has been known variously as avant-garde, off-West-End, underground, alternative or non-mainstream theatre. It is certainly the alternative to traditional commercial theatre. It takes place in studio theatres, in the back rooms of pubs, in attics, cellars and warehouses, in large rooms, in any open space, even in the streets. It is amateur; it is professional. Standards of performance and production range from the atrocious to the polished. Its location, subject matter, times of performance and scale of production contrast sharply with the traditional theatre-based presentation of plays.

The fringe groups which appeared in the late 1960s were the logical successors to the small private club theatres which operated in the immediate post-war period, mainly in London, such as the New Lindsey, the Mercury, the Boltons and the Watergate. Here, under club conditions, were presented plays banned by the Lord Chamberlain from public performance because of taboo subjects, forbidden language or violence. But unlike the new fringe theatres, such club theatres presented mainly full-length plays on a traditional, though tiny, stage and often in a conventional production.

Modern fringe theatre could be said to continue the work of these private club theatres, or it could be traced to the 'fringe' companies which clustered around the main attractions at the Edinburgh Festival, referred to in the title of the revue *Beyond the Fringe,* which opened in 1960. Such companies operated occasionally, and the concept of year-round fringe theatre had not then been considered. But by 1968 the American influence had been felt and the pace had accelerated, fringe theatre had become a regular activity. It was a year of student riots at the Sorbonne, anti-Vietnam demonstrations at Berkeley and Columbia Universities in America, and disrupted classes and occupied buildings at the London School of Economics. The students were protesting against political, social and educational ways of life which they considered were unsatisfactory and in need of radical reappraisal. This was a time when creative pop musicians such as the Beatles and the Rolling Stones were in their heyday, and experiments in rock opera produced shows like *Tommy* by *The Who.* Drug culture had spread and young people were forging their own permissive lifestyle. A loose, strident, violent musical stage offered them a theatre of protest, and they seized it with shocking abandon.

However, not all these activities were political or presented by students. Certain professional theatre groups were formed about this time, many of which, like the Pip Simmons Group and the People Show, continued to operate professionally up to the 1980s, offering alternative, experimental shows. A few of these groups have joined the political protest movement, for instance 7:84 and Red Ladder Theatre (formerly Agitprop). (The 7:84 company is so named after

The People Show, a fringe group (formed in 1965) used shock tactics, nonsense and partly improvised their performances. This is *People Show No. 82* at the Bush Theatre.

their claim that 7 per cent of the British population owns 84 per cent of the country's wealth.) The Red Ladder group began by specialising in plays dealing with land speculation, property development and housing problems, all treated in a semi-documentary way and tinged with Marxist commitment.

John MacGrath, who founded 7:84, had the declared objective of raising political consciousness, primarily of the working class and its potential allies. David Edgar continued the trend in the 1970s with his manifesto of radical, alternative, Marxist theatre. Many such playwrights declared that their socialist, realist plays were expressly intended to precipitate social change. Howard Barker declared that the stage 'is the last remaining arena for the free assault of our society'. The shock tactics and aggression were self-confessed. David Hare remarked in 1972, 'Our aggressiveness is immensely conscious. I suppose it stems from a basic contempt for people who go to the theatre. We wanted to pick up the medium of theatre and shake it by the scruff of its neck.' Even a non-fringe playwright like Joe Orton declared, 'One *must* shake the audience out of its expectations. They need not so much shocking, as surprising out of their rut.'

Fringe theatre has become less aggressive and is now a more or less respectable alternative to mainstream theatre, though its activities still remain astonishingly varied. The provision of a second, smaller theatre-space in most newly-built provincial theatres is an acknowledgement that this new alternative drama is playing a vital part in the theatrical life of the country and needs its own non-traditional presentation-space. Alternative productions are also a regular feature of the work of the Royal Shakespeare Company, the National Theatre and the Royal Court Theatre, which all possess special studio space. The theatre-going public regularly attend and are prepared to accept the bare essentials of a small-scale production, and a reduction in auditorium comforts which they would not have been satisfied with in the 1960s.

the writer today

Throughout most of theatre history the playwright has been the key figure providing the all-important script. However today the playwright's pre-eminence is being questioned: it has been discovered that a play can be created by actors themselves, in workshop conditions, without a prepared written script. Many groups indulge in this kind of 'play-writing', though none has been as successful as Mike Leigh and his actors, who have shown both on stage and on television that actors can improvise and themselves write a rich and rewarding play. A topic is chosen and each individual actor decides and then develops his own 'character'; the characters are then brought together in a given situation and, from a period of intense improvised rehearsals, a play is distilled.

Such a production was *Abigail's Party*, seen at the Hampstead Theatre in 1977, and *Goose Pimples,* which reached the West End in 1981. Improvisatory drama, both as an aid to the realisation of a scripted play and as an end-product in its own right, is now common practice, and while the standards attained by most groups may not equal the fiercely dedicated efforts of Mike Leigh and his players, nor indeed the skilled writing of an Ayckbourn, Stoppard, Bond or Shaffer, nevertheless such techniques are producing interesting work.

Modern drama's interest in non-verbal theatre is also nibbling away at the status of 'the word', so long the essence of any play. An increased use of mime, music, ritual and even silence can be observed. Such non-verbal elements, with consequent reduction in the importance of dialogue and words, are seen in such early plays as Wesker's *Chips with Everything* (1962), in the raid on the coal store – an entire scene without a line being spoken. Other examples of non-verbal theatre are found in David Storey's *The Contractor* (1969), during which a marquee is erected and dismantled on stage in full view of the audience, and in his *Changing Room* (1972), a play with no plot, which shows a rugby team dressing and undressing on-stage for an off-stage game. In more recent plays, especially in fringe theatre, music and songs are freely introduced, and dialogue is restricted to very basic language indeed – complete with long pauses – as though speeches of more than a few words are to be avoided at all costs. The tolerance of profanity in stage dialogue, and previously 'forbidden' words, is further symptomatic of the decline in the literary quality of plays; actions speak louder than words.

Fringe playwrights were writing for an audience who had never been to a theatre. So the theatre had to come to them in the form of touring shows visiting village halls, community centres, working men's clubs, sit-ins and strikes at factories – even in the street. Such audiences were unused to literary lyricism; a tale must be plainly told. In addition, since the objective was usually political activism, the message must be simple in order to get it across. The concentration on movement, dance, mime, sound and lighting effects led to this displacement of 'the word' from its previous pre-eminent position.

Sizwe Bansi is Dead by Athol Fugard at the Royal Court in 1974.
Fugard is a white South African dramatist whose immensely
respected plays are regularly performed in Britain.

The documentary play has further minimised the need
for a playwright. Most documentary drama is the result of
group activity, and has been especially successful and popular
at regional repertory theatres where the entire company,
under the leadership of the artistic director, researches and
creates a play. Pioneering work of this kind has been done by
Peter Cheeseman at the Victoria Theatre, Stoke-on-Trent,
compiling such plays as *The Knotty* (1969), on the building of
the North Staffordshire Railway; *Six Into One* (1970), on the
amalgamation and reorganisation of six local towns into the
one city of Stoke-on-Trent; and *The Fight for Shelton Bar*

(1974), the dramatisation of a local industrial dispute. *Close the Coalhouse Door*, compiled by Alan Plater at Newcastle-on-Tyne and based on the decline of the coal industry in the north-east, was so successful that it achieved a London showing.

emphasis on the director

The practice of 'devising' a play and not relying solely on the playwright to provide the script has greatly increased the importance of the director. In recognition of this fact, theatre today is often described as director's theatre, and this is confirmed by the habitual reference to Peter Brook's production of the *Marat-Sade*, of the Marowitz *Hamlet* and Trevor Nunn's *The Comedy of Errors*, where strong directorial influence was manifest and the playwright's name unmentioned. The emphasis today is often on the director's interpretation of a play and less on the playwright's intentions.

A vast amount of experimental work has been done on the staging of drama and there are few fundamental approaches left unexplored. A modern director is generally concerned with uncovering the theme of a play and discovering how best to present it. However, there are certain extremely gifted directors who have the knack of suddenly presenting a play in an unusual (though effective) manner in a setting or style never previously considered. Such, for instance, was Peter Brook's 1970 production of Shakespeare's *A Midsummer Night's Dream* acted out on a stage which resembled a completely empty large white box – rather like a squash court. Gone was any hint of Athens; there was no sign of a tree; certain characters spent a lot of time on swinging trapezes, others indulged in spinning plates on the ends of rods like Chinese jugglers, and Titania's bower was a huge flame-coloured bed of ostrich feathers. Surely this was a totally unsuitable setting for such a romantic play which involved the fairies and a mischievous sprite called Puck? But somehow it worked. Actors manipulated coiled springs of wire to represent the trees in the forest; the spinning plates were the love charms; and the costumes, like simple nightdresses or

The Glasgow Citizens' Theatre has built up a reputation for its exciting approach to the classics. Above is a scene from *Hamlet*, directed by Robert MacDonald.

plain trousers and tops, allowed the audience to make of them what they wished. The result was that an all too familiar play suddenly had a fresh new look.

Peter Brook is without question the most brilliant and inventive director in the theatre today. He has directed many productions in the commercial theatre and for the Royal Shakespeare Company. He has set up his own workshops both in England and latterly in Paris, where he has sought to discover new ways of 'communicating' through theatre. He wrote in the magazine *Encore* as early as 1961, 'I believe in the word in classical drama, because the word was their tool. I do not believe in the word much today, because it has outlived

Oberon (Alan Howard) and Puck (John Kane) in Peter Brook's production of *A Midsummer Night's Dream* (RSC 1970).

its purpose. Words do not communicate, they do not express much, and most of the time they fail abysmally to define.' In 1968 in his book *The Empty Space* he continued, 'Is there another language, just as exciting for the author, as a language of words?' Later he attempted to find the answer to this with an open-air production of *Orghast at Persepolis* (1971), set amid the desert and rocks of Iran; mime, spectacle and the sound of a new tongue (specially created by the poet Ted Hughes) replaced conventional language and action. Since then his productions have included *IK* (presented at The Roundhouse in 1979) evoking by force of acting alone (without scenery, make-up or costume) the plight of an African tribe dying from starvation, and an extraordinary production of Chekhov's *The Cherry Orchard* (1981) in the abandoned theatre which is his Paris workshop, where the action wandered throughout the building.

Chief among the gifted directors working today for the National Theatre and the Royal Shakespeare Company is Peter Hall. In 1960, at the age of thirty, he took over as Director of the RSC and in 1973 he succeeded Laurence Olivier as Director of the National Theatre. A person of great administrative as well as artistic capability, Peter Hall has worked in theatre, opera and films. He is perhaps best associated with contemporary drama and is the acknowledged interpreter of the work of Harold Pinter with whom he has had a close association. Hall had notable success with his 1981 production of *The Oresteia,* the classic Greek tragedy made up of three plays, which was performed in its entirety. It was played in masks by an all-male cast using a new translation which was spoken to musical accompaniment, mainly percussion. It proved to be an extraordinary piece of theatre.

While Peter Hall has never evolved any specific hallmarks in his productions, those of John Dexter, however, have a certain panache and visual splendour. He made his name as a director with the English Stage Company (ESC) in the 1950s and 1960s before joining the National Theatre. At the ESC he was closely associated with the plays of Arnold Wesker. His magnificent production of *The Royal Hunt of the Sun* (1964), which played Chichester, the Old Vic and on Broadway in America, is unforgettable. Dexter will also be remembered for

his productions of the French classics – Molière's *The
Misanthrope* and *Phaedra Britannica* (after Racine); for an
excitingly staged *Equus* which had members of the public on-
stage acting as a kind of jury to the play; and most recently for
a hugely successful version of Brecht's *The Life of Galileo*
which established Michael Gambon as a rising star. John
Dexter has the reputation in the profession of staging the
unstageable and he pioneered devices which are now common stage-practice, such as leaving visible the bare walls of
the stage and using metal and polystyrene for stage-scenery.

emphasis
on the
director

When Peter Hall left the RSC he was succeeded by
Trevor Nunn. The bulk of Nunn's expertise has been gained
in directing Shakespeare and other Renaissance playwrights.
The RSC in the 1960s and 1970s had a particular 'house-style'
of production – a strong physical acting presence and a striking visual scenic element. This was abundantly evident in
Nunn's 1967 production of Tourneur's *The Revenger's
Tragedy* at Stratford-upon-Avon, a brilliantly effective
interpretation of this macabre revenge play. He has been
responsible for many other memorable productions – a striking blood-red staging of *Macbeth* and an enchanting and hila-
rious version of *The Comedy of Errors,* set in a sun-ridden,
vaguely Greek, junta state ruled by generals in dark glasses,
and with a teeming open-air nightlife in the local square complete with outdoor film show. Nunn also staged the phe-
nomenally successful *Nicholas Nickleby* in both London and
New York.

There are many other important directors working in
the English theatre today, but lack of space prevents full dis-
cussion of their work. However, their names at least should be
recorded (in alphabetical order): John Barton, Michael
Blakemore, Michael Bogdanov, Bill Bryden, John Caird, Ron
Daniels, Frank Dunlop, Ronald Eyre, William Gaskill, Peter
Gill, Terry Hands, David Jones, Donald McWhinnie, Clifford
Williams, Peter Wood.

One continental director whose work deserves comment is Jerzy Grotowski, born in Poland in 1933. While most of
the directors so far discussed have revolutionised the 'look' of
a production – by exciting lighting, magnificent and unusual
settings, revitalised acting – or have presented the play in

A scene from *The Speakers* (actor Tony Rohr; director Bill Gaskell) presented by Joint Stock Theatre Company, an established touring fringe theatre group.

such a way that its 'message' has been readily transmitted, none has tackled a play in quite the same way Grotowski does. For him, drama is a confrontation between the actor and audience. Like many early directors, Grotowski trains the actor to be physically supple like a gymnast; he also adds an essence – a trance-like spirituality – so that an audience cannot help but respond to such an overwhelming physical and spiritual presence.

**emphasis
on the
director**

Grotowski does not present his productions in a conventional theatre; his acting arena may be a simple large room or small hall, and audience numbers are severely restricted. Furthermore he adapts the plays he presents, offering what he feels is the essence of the play in question; for instance, Marlowe's *Dr Faustus* which he directed in 1963 is limited to only Faustus and Mephistophilis. The manner of presentation is carefully devised and there is no stage in the usual sense. *Dr Faustus* is played as though the audience were attending a supper with Faustus, sitting at long low refectory tables placed in a π shape. The audience occupies seats at the tables; the action is performed on the table tops. In his version of Calderon's play *The Constant Prince,* presented in 1965, the audience observed the play performed on a slightly lower level – as though they were observers in an operating theatre. Such productions are powerful pieces of theatre, although set in circumstances which preclude them from commercial application.

In his book *Towards a Poor Theatre* (1969) Grotowski attempts to explain his views on theatre. Clearly Grotowski's approach is a singular one (it has been described as mystic). Nevertheless his dedication to the theatrical experience must be acknowledged, and his work, rich in ritual and starkly effective, has attracted many devotees, especially of his actor-training programmes.

Perhaps the most celebrated American director is Lee Strasberg (1901–82), already noted as the founder of the New York Actors' Studio and inventor of the Method school of acting. Like Grotowski, Strasberg's influence in the field of production has been in the sphere of acting, where the strength and vitality of the performer have been the core of any production. More recently, the American director Harold

**emphasis
on the
director**

Prince (b. 1928) has become known on this side of the Atlantic for his snappy productions of American and English musicals – or rather plays with music. He established himself with *Cabaret* in 1968 (which later became an award-winning film), following this with *Company* (1970) and *Candide* (1973), before coming to England to direct Andrew Lloyd Webber's *Evita* (1978) and *Sweeny Todd* (1979).

summing up

The last twenty-five to thirty years have seen many changes in the theatre. The convention of the 'well-made play', a carefully structured three- or four-act play of exposition, development, complication and dénouement, with its dialogue of literary pretension and its neat solution of problems at curtain fall, has crumbled. We now have a two-part play with one interval, offering colloquial dialogue and a final scene which is inconclusive and open-ended. There is growing interest in the lives and problems not of the upper classes but of the lower classes. The audience's isolation has been shattered; it now finds itself in the middle of the action, often physically, always metaphorically; it is assailed by non-verbal images and occasionally subject to direct address from the actors. Stars and the playwright are no longer pre-eminent; the accent is on teamwork and collaboration. Official censorship has gone, leaving the stage free to discuss life's most unlikely problems.

Fringe theatre has mushroomed and with it a rash of politically committed drama. The giants of the National Theatre and the Royal Shakespeare Company have emerged, each contributing in its individual way to keeping Britain at the pinnacle of the theatrical world. Regional repertory companies have flourished, many of them in new theatres – as at Birmingham, Colchester, Harlow, Leeds, Lancaster, Sheffield, Swindon and Manchester.

It has been a period of 'brilliant confusion' as one critic has termed it. A confusion occasioned by the sheer volume and variety of drama available.

stage
and
auditorium
shapes

In the first half of this century all public theatres were very much the same; some were more grand than others of course, but all of them invariably had proscenium-arch stages. Today there is no such uniformity. New approaches to play presentation over the last few decades have resulted in a variety of shapes of both stage and auditorium. New theatre buildings reflect such change.

proscenium-arch stage
(usually termed *pros. arch*)

Most theatres in use today belong to this group and were probably built in the late nineteenth or early twentieth century, hence the term 'traditional'. The over-all shape is rectangular with a raised stage placed squarely across one end stretching from side wall to side wall. The proscenium-arch is a square or oblong opening in the wall which separates the auditorium from the stage, through which the audience views the play. A proscenium-arch stage is also called a *picture frame stage*.

The Victorian elegance of the Lyric Theatre, Hammersmith, London, renowned in the '40s and '50s for its productions by H. M. Tennant and the 59 Theatre Company. Destroyed in 1965 for a redevelopment scheme it was rebuilt in 1979, complete with Victorian plasterwork decor and an added Studio theatre.

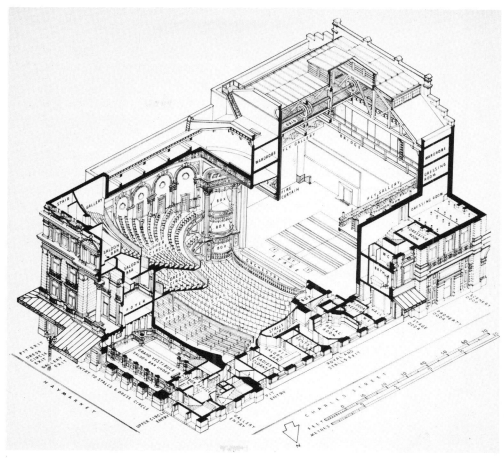

Richard Leacroft's splendid scale reconstruction drawing of Her
Majesty's Theatre, Haymarket, rebuilt 1897. It was the first theatre in
Britain to be built with a flat stage. Outlines on the stage indicate the
trapdoors and cuts (sections of the stage-floor which slid away to
enable scenery/actors to rise from below).

In more modern theatres where there is no proscenium-arch but where the stage is placed across the end of a
rectangular auditorium, the term *end-staging* is used. Yet
another term for pros. arch staging is *fourth-wall* theatre, since
an audience is observing the action (in interior scenes)
through the imagined fourth wall of that setting.

The strength of pros. arch staging lies in its potential
to offer a striking approximation of realism in scenic terms.
Indeed, this form of staging is often referred to as the *scenic-
stage*, and some marvellous representations on stage can be
created of both indoor and outdoor scenes. Since the play is
end-staged all members of the audience receive the same
visual and dramatic effects.

However, the stage may be a long way from certain parts of the house (auditorium) — especially the upper circle and gallery — and, to be really effective, it requires dressing with scenery which is expensive to build and takes time and many stage-hands to set and change. Furthermore, this scenic stage is unsuitable for many modern plays, most of which are written in short scenes with the action taking place at a number of different locations. Some critics believe that the pros. arch and its attendant orchestra pit create an artificial barrier between actor and audience which makes audience involvement and participation difficult, and it is also felt that the sheer size of many traditional theatre-buildings is unsuitable for the more intimate modern drama.

When a play's action spills out in front of the pros. arch, it will be on a stage belonging to the next group.

thrust stage or promontory stage

Most pros. arch stages possess a strip of stage in front of the house tabs (main curtain) on which action can take place. The traditional name for this is the *fore-stage*, so called since Restoration times to distinguish it from the scenic-stage which was well upstage and in which little or no action took place. By the late nineteenth century the stage had contracted in depth and the scenic and acting stage had merged into one. The term fore-stage is still used to denote the stage area in front of the house tabs, but the more commonly used expression for it is the *apron*.

The term *thrust stage* (or, occasionally, *promontory stage*) is used where the stage is considerably extended into the auditorium and most of the action takes place on it. In old theatres, a thrust stage is often the result of an attempt to ignore the pros. arch in the process of modernising the theatre. The thrust stage came to prominence in the 1950s with the placing of the action among and not merely in front of the audience. In thrust-stage theatres the audience is placed around the stage on three sides.

By thrusting the action into the audience, the promoters of this form of staging claim that the action is more immediate and the audience more readily involved. The actors are less restricted in movement and position *vis-à-vis* the audience (the pros. arch stage requires the actors to spend most of their time facing the audience), and by playing against a background rather than within it the need for a full stage-setting is reduced.

On pronounced thrust-stages, however, an actor will have difficulty in finding a spot from which to command the entire house and, inevitably, some of the audience, some of the time, will be faced with the backs of actors.

This form of staging has been adopted by many new British theatres. An outstanding example is the Crucible Theatre, Sheffield, which opened in 1971.

traverse staging

This is not a very common form of staging and is more suitable for pageants and fashion-show parades than for traditional drama. Large halls or chambers not regularly used as public performance-areas may be adapted in this way.

Traverse staging can sometimes be employed with startlingly good results in modern theatres. The stage divides the audience in half and is placed transversely down the length or across the breadth of the auditorium. The actors play either on a raised stage or at floor level, with the audience seating raked.

Traverse staging is ideal for pageants, shows, large-cast plays, comedies and plays involving a lot of movement. It is unsuitable for serious, static, small-cast plays. When used, scenic elements have to be restricted to the two end extremities of the stage.

arena staging or theatre-in-the-round

Here, the audience surrounds the acting area. The term derives from the Latin *harena* meaning 'sand' or 'a sandy place' – a reference to the arena in which gladiatorial combats, circuses and similar activities took place in ancient

Rome. The term *arena-staging* is perhaps more applicable to very large-scale theatrical presentations, both indoors and out.

In smaller theatres the term most commonly used is *theatre-in-the-round*. ('Round' refers to the fact that the audience surrounds the acting area, not that the stage is circular in shape; most are polygonal or rectangular.) Such auditoria are small, seating only a few hundred people. There are not many theatres in Britain or on the Continent indulging exclusively in this kind of presentation. The most notable in Britain are the Library Theatre, Scarborough (the first such theatre in Britain), the Victoria Theatre, Stoke-on-Trent, and the Round House, London. The first purpose-built permanent theatre-in-the-round is The Royal Exchange Theatre, Manchester, which opened in 1976. Many modern theatres, though not designed

Manchester's *Royal Exchange Theatre* showing the stage and central lighting basket; the first permanent *purpose-built* 'in-the-round' theatre in England. Conceived by Richard Negri it opened September 1976.

as theatres-in-the-round, are capable of adaptation to this form of staging.

Advocates of theatre-in-the-round assert that it creates a much more vital and immediate performance for an audience than is possible in a traditional theatre. It concentrates the audience's attention on the reality of the actor's performance (making, incidentally, his job more demanding). Virtually no scenery is possible, so that environment and atmosphere on stage are difficult to achieve. Floor surfaces (the audience looks down on the stage), furniture and costume therefore assume great importance. Lighting is used to 'paint' much of the visual effect.

The major disadvantage is that the audience will not always see the action from the best viewpoint, and will also have to contend with the actors' backs for approximately half the performance. This form of staging imposes constant movement on a production which may well not suit the play. It can also be difficult to stage certain specific pieces of action and to decide where and how to arrange vital pieces of furniture – as in a 'discovery scene' or a court-room scene. Economically, this form of staging has obvious advantages over the picture-frame stage, which no doubt often influences a decision to adopt it.

open stage

The *open-stage* is a direct result of the anti-illusionist approach to drama of the 1960s of bringing the action out into the open from behind the pros. arch, and of exposing the mechanics of theatre.

An open-stage implies a thrust-stage or at least a convex shape curving out into the auditorium. Most modern theatres have abandoned the traditional rectangular shaped theatre-building and adopted a polygonal shape. The most favoured shape seems to be the hexagon or the octagon (the Octagon Theatre at Bolton, Lancashire is precisely and aptly so named). Within the polygonal shape, an open stage is set in one of its corners, the stage shape itself being a polygon. A raked fan-shaped auditorium looks down upon it. Other good examples are the Chichester Festival Theatre (1962), the Leeds Playhouse (1970) and the Olivier Theatre at the National (1976).

The open thrust stage is Shakespeare's stage and is not far from the shape of the Greek stage. It therefore offers splendid opportunities for the production of classic plays, and by doing away with the pros. arch and orchestra-pit barrier, it also conforms to the modern concept of a close actor/audience relationship. Theatres with open thrust stages vary in size from those with a large seating capacity (like the examples given above) to the more modest stages of regional repertory theatres like the Key Theatre at Peterborough and the Redgrave Theatre at Farnham. On these smaller open thrust stages, nineteenth-century and early twentieth-century plays which require full scenic sets present no problem, which they might do if attempted on larger stages.

Most recently-built theatres have adopted the open thrust stage with audience capacities of between four and five hundred.

totally variable/adjustable stage

This implies the ability to radically alter the presentation arrangement by rapidly and smoothly operating mechanical means. There are several such theatres in America (on university campuses) but only one in Britain – the New London Theatre built in 1973. Most theatres are capable of altering slightly the shape and size of the stage; it is comparatively easy, for instance, to add a fore-stage to a pros. arch stage. In practice it has been found very costly, and perhaps an unwarrantable luxury, to have a theatre equipped with a mechanically-controlled completely variable and adjustable stage.

glossary

Acts Main division of a play, like a chapter in a book. Acts are further divided into *scenes* (q.v.). Act division stems from the original classical Greek practice of dividing a tragedy into four or five alternating episodes and choral odes. In English drama, plays were not regularly structured into Acts and scenes until after the Renaissance. By the nineteenth century it was customary for the 'well-made-play' to have four or five Acts.

Agit-Prop Short for 'agitational propaganda'. Agit-Prop theatre is usually politically orientated and expressly designed to 'stir things up'.

Allegory A literary term denoting a narrative description of a subject which suggests another by its similarity. In plays, the action and the characters are suggestive of (and make comment upon) other similar actions and characters. For example, Miller's play *The Crucible,* set in seventeenth-century Salem, Massachusetts and concerning witchcraft, is an allegory of Senator McCarthy's political witch-hunts in the United States in the 1940s and 1950s.

Alternative theatre   The opposite of traditional theatre. It denotes theatre that is *not* performed in a traditional manner on a proscenium-arch stage. Other names for such theatre are: fringe, underground, non-mainstream, off-off-Broadway, off-West-End theatre.

Angels   Financial backers who provide producers with the money to help stage a theatrical production. They are prepared to lose their money if the show is unsuccessful but recover their money and reap a fair dividend if the show succeeds.

The apron   Modern term for the extreme front part of a stage in front of the curtain line and the proscenium arch.

Arena stage   The type of staging in which the audience surrounds the acting area. From the Latin *harena* meaning 'sand' or a 'sandy place' – a reference to the arena in which gladiatorial combats or circuses took place in ancient Rome (see Chapter 6).

Aside   Technical term for an actor's remarks meant to be heard by the audience but *not* by his fellow actors on stage.

ASM   Assistant stage manager (see Chapter 4).

Back-stage   The entire area behind the proscenium arch (other than the stage) – the dressing rooms, prop rooms, wardrobe, green room, etc., areas inhabited by the cast and stage crews. A **back-stage worker** is a non-actor member of a company, involved technically in wardrobe, properties, carpenter's shop, etc., or a member of the stage crew.

Beginners   This does *not* mean those who have just started in the profession. 'Beginners please' is called by the SM or ASM just before 'curtain up' to warn those members of the cast who appear in the opening scene.

Blocking   The process of arranging the actors' moves on stage. At an early rehearsal the director will 'block' the play, indicating the positions of the cast on stage, their exits and entrances, when and where they are to move and in which chairs they are to sit, etc., during their scenes on stage.

Boards

Colloquial expression for 'the stage', derived from the practice of using boards or planks to make a stage floor. 'He is on the boards' means he is an actor.

Borders

Strips of scenic cloth hung above the stage in rows one behind the other, parallel to the front of the stage. They not only complete the stage picture in terms of scenery but mask off the stage roof.

Box set

A complete stage setting representing an interior scene, i.e. a drawing room, dining room, lounge, etc., Box sets are composed of a continuous number of stage-flats (q.v.) joined together and arranged around the three sides of a stage with the 'fourth wall' of the room being represented (i.e. that between the stage and the auditorium) missing. Box sets come complete with ceilings, ornaments, pictures, etc., and are fully furnished. Today, they are becoming increasingly rare on stage, and the vogue is for an *indication* only and not a complete *representation* of an interior setting.

Braces

These support and keep upright the stage flats (q.v.). Braces are expandable wooden fittings, like an expanding rigid ruler, with hooks at each end which engage in eye hooks in the flats and in stage weights on the floor, thus keeping the flats rigid and upright.

Call

A notification – either via a loudspeaker system, by a notice on the call-board or by letter – that one's presence is required for a rehearsal, a photo-call, a costume-fitting, a company meeting, etc., or to stand by for one's next entrance on stage during a performance.

Cyc
(pronounced 'syke')

Abbreviated from 'cyclorama' – a floor-to-ceiling scenic canvas backcloth stretched across the back of the stage. It can be lit in a variety of ways, either decoratively or to represent the open sky; cloud, fog or rain effects, etc., can be projected on it. Often the plain whitewashed back wall of the stage is used instead of a cyc.

Dark	'The theatre is dark' means that it is temporarily shut. A dark week in a theatre's programme is when no show is booked to play that particular week.
Discovered	Apart from its obvious meaning that a performer suddenly receives recognition and subsequent star billing, 'discovered' means that an actor is already on stage when the curtain goes up or the action starts.
Director	The person who directs a production, guiding, advising, and encouraging the actors in their performances and the *interpreter* of a play, who has artistic control over what is presented on stage. Not to be confused with the producer (q.v.) (see Chapter 4).
Double bill	Two short plays or two substantial items of entertainment, presented as an evening's programme instead of the more usual single full-length play or item.
DSM	Deputy stage manager (see Chapter 4).
Down-stage	That part of the stage nearest the audience (in a proscenium-arch theatre). The term is derived from the perspective stage of the fifteenth-century Italian theatre, the level of which inclined sharply towards the back.
Duologue	Dialogue (stage conversation between two people only).
Ensemble acting	Acting by a company in which no single actor attempts to outshine the others, but all work together to make the most of the play they are presenting.
Experimental theatre	Implies a highly unconventional interpretation of a play, i.e. a novel form of presentation or an unusual treatment of the text.
Expressionism	An attempt to represent on stage a 'state of mind' or the inner life of humanity, rather than its natural outward everyday reality. The expressionist movement originated at the turn of the twentieth century with Strindberg and the German playwrights, especially Toller and Wedekind.

174

Fit up A production *not* presented in a regular theatre building but in a space 'fitted out' with a temporary stage and fittings.

Flats Rectangular pieces of scenery, usually oblong in shape and of standard sizes ranging from 4 to 8 feet wide and anything from 8 to 10 feet, or 18 to 30 feet high. They are wooden framed and covered on one side with canvas which is then painted.

Flies The area high above the stage, more specifically the **fly gallery,** which is fixed high up to the walls surrounding the stage and gives access to stage machinery, particularly flying equipment operated by **fly-men.** A **fly mechanism** raises and lowers pieces of scenery, usually by means of a counterweight system.

Floats Originally lighted wicks floating in troughs of oil which provided stage lighting. They were placed along the leading edge of the stage and were later replaced, first with gas, and then electric lights and called 'footlights'. Footlights are now rarely fitted to stages.

Floods Stage lights or lanterns giving a broad flood of illumination; they are basically a bulb in a metal box with a reflector.

FOH Front of house; can also be termed 'out front'. Refers to the theatre's auditorium, foyers, etc., i.e. everything on the spectator's side of the proscenium arch. FOH has its own staff, separate from the back-stage staff.

Fold If a show folds, it ends. 'Fold' usually implies a very short run and suggests a failure. If a successful show ends after a satisfactory but limited run of performances it does not 'fold' but 'closes'.

Fore-stage Since the Restoration, the traditional name for the down-stage, front part of a stage. In modern times it means the area in front of the curtain and nearest the audience. Also called 'the apron' (q.v.).

Fourth-wall convention	The convention that an audience watching a play is observing life in a room with the fourth wall (that between stage and auditorium) removed.
Fringe	See *Alternative theatre* and Chapter 12.
Get-in	The date and time when a new production's scenery and equipment, etc. are admitted to the theatre, and the process of setting-up begins. The get-in is dependent on the dismantling (striking) and evacuation of the previous show's scenery and equipment (the 'get-out'), leaving a clear stage for the incoming production.
Get-out figure	The figure of gross weekly box office takings, agreed between producer and theatre-lessee, below which the takings must not fall if the play is to be retained at that theatre.
The Gods	Refers to the cheapest seats in the gallery at the back of the theatre. Their occupants are also sometimes referred to collectively as 'the Gods', implying those high up! (The equivalent French term is *paradis* and its occupants are *les enfants du paradis*.)
'Going up'	The usual theatrical cry back-stage when the play is about to start, i.e. the curtain is going up.
Green room	The actors' back-stage common-room, where they can relax when not on-stage and can see visitors. Originally so called in the late seventeenth century as it was invariably decorated in green. It was the room in which the actors, and especially the actresses, received their admirers.
Grid	Gridiron. A strong steel/iron framework or grid set high above the stage, primarily used for securing a system of pulleys and lines (steel cables) to which scenery can be attached and raised and lowered ('flown') and which also supports the borders (q.v.).
Groundlings	Term used by Shakespeare in *Hamlet* (and in general use at that time) to refer to the audience members who stood in the Pit (on the ground), the cheapest place in the Elizabethan theatre. Hence also implies an unrefined or uncritical person.

Ground-row	A long low piece of scenery (free-standing), usually resembling a low mound, a bank of flowers, a small fence, etc.
The half	The latest time by which an actor in a play must arrive at the theatre – half-an-hour before curtain-up. (In fact it is thirty-five minutes before, since beginners (q.v.) are called five minutes before the advertised start of the play.)
Heavens	An Elizabethan/Jacobean term referring to the underside (visible to the audience) of the large canopy over the otherwise open stage. This underside was thought to have been elaborately painted with stars, clouds, etc., to resemble 'the heavens'.
Heroic tragedy	English form of drama in vogue in the late seventeenth century, usually written in rhymed couplets and dealing with themes of love and honour. Dryden was its greatest exponent.
The house	The auditorium of the theatre, or the audience, 'Who's in the house?' means which VIP's are among the audience? 'Papering the house' means filling the seats with complimentary (free) ticket holders; 'How's the house?' means how big or how responsive is the audience?
House style	A particular style or approach denoting, and associated with a specific theatrical company.
House tabs	See *Tabs*.
Iambic pentameter	Literary term to describe the metre of a specific line of poetry which regularly has five stressed and five unstressed syllables, e.g. 'If music be the food of love, play on'. Used by Shakespeare and most other Renaissance playwrights.
Ice	American theatrical term referring to surcharges on ticket prices. When, over and above legitimate ticket agency fees, a further surcharge (of an illegal and exorbitant nature) is added to the standard ticket price, such excess payment is 'ice'.

Impresario	Person who organises and presents (i.e. produces) public entertainment for commercial gain.
Impro-visatory theatre	The result of improvisation by the actors. Such a play is unscripted, though the general scenario may be roughly agreed on beforehand; the performance is entirely the result of the actors responding to each other on the spur of the moment. The technique of improvisation is often used by a playwright 'in residence' and a cast, in the process of creating a play.
The iron	The safety curtain. The term derives from the fact that the safety curtain is made from an incombustible material with a steel framework. It can be lowered to block off the stage from the auditorium thus creating a fire-break between back-stage and front-of-house. 'Drop the iron' means lowering ('letting in') the safety curtain.
Legitimate theatre	('Legit.' for short.) Has nothing to do with distinguishing between an honest and a 'shady' theatre management, but refers to the presentation of plays (drama) as opposed to variety theatre, musicals, shows, etc. 'He's legit.' means he is a straight actor, not a variety or music-hall artist, and not primarily a dancer, singer or comedian. The term dates back to the seventeenth century when only the two patent theatres holding the monopoly were allowed to present straight drama – hence legitimate theatre (see Chapter 9).
Legs	Pairs of full-length heavy drapes hanging on either side of the stage (usually some four or five pairs are used) to mask off the wings (q.v.).
Limes	Very powerful spotlights usually operated from high up at the back of the theatre. They are able to pick out a solo artist in a circle of light and follow him/her around the stage. So named after the source of the light – an intense white light produced by heating a piece of lime in an oxyhydrogen flame.
Line-up	The arrangement of the cast as they take their curtain-call after a performance. They 'line up' parallel to the front of the stage with the leading actors occupying centre-stage.

Mask   'To mask off' means to hide the back-stage areas by arranging drapes or scenery in such a way that the audience cannot see into the wings. If an actor is 'masked' on stage it means he is hidden (or partially hidden) from the audience, either by another actor or by a piece of scenery or furniture.

MD   Musical director.

Metaphor   A name or descriptive term given to an object or person – clearly defining it – but to which such a name or term cannot literally be applied. E.g. in *Othello*, Iago speaks of the relationship between Othello the Moor and the white Desdemona as 'an old black ram is tupping your white ewe'.

Naturalism   In theatre, the attempt to achieve on-stage performances and productions which seem entirely natural, without artifice or conscious effort, and totally in accordance with the world as we daily experience it.

Open stage   A stage with no proscenium arch which is open on its sides and front. 'Open stage' implies that it is a thrust stage of some kind.

Out front   If an actor is told to deliver a line 'out front' it means direct to the audience. As a general term 'out front' means in the audience or auditorium.

Panatrope   Record player and amplification equipment, part of a theatre's sound equipment found in the control room and operated by the SM or ASM.

Pass door   The door giving direct access from back-stage to front-of-house. It can be found near the proscenium arch and will probably be labelled 'strictly private'.

Picture-frame stage   Another name for the proscenium arch stage (q.v.).

Preview performances   Public performances given before the official 'first night'.

Producer	The person who arranges for a play or show's presentation/production. His concern is administrative and financial, not artistic. Not to be confused with the director (q.v.) (see Chapter 4).
Promenade performances	A recent innovation in theatre presentation, where the audience is not seated but free to move about during the play's action. Often in promenade performances the actors perform among the audience, moving through them to different locations in the acting area. The audience literally follows the action.
PS or Prompt side	Stage-left. The left-hand side of the stage by the proscenium arch was the traditional place from which the play used to be prompted during a performance.
Props	Short for 'properties'. There are two kinds; stage and hand. **Stage props** are the ornaments, pictures, vases, china and crockery, etc., which furnish a stage setting – everything other than scenery and furniture. **Hand props** are those used by the cast during the performance, e.g. documents, cigarette lighters, attache cases, walking sticks, and so on. The **props table** for such hand props is arranged conveniently in the wings; the cast collects props from and returns them to this table. The **props man** provides or makes the required props.
Proscenium arch	The term is derived from the Greek *pro-skenion;* the equivalent in the modern theatre is the large rectangular opening in the wall which separates the stage from the auditorium and which frames the audience's view of a performance.
Rep or Repertory theatre	Strictly speaking, this means a theatre with a resident company of performers offering in rotation a number of plays from its repertoire, so that in any one week several different plays can be presented on successive evenings. Such companies include the National Theatre and the Royal Shakespeare Company. Today the term has come to mean a resident acting company of a set number of players who, during a season, present a succession of productions each lasting for about three weeks.

Revival	A fresh production of a play which has been staged before.
Running time	The length of time it takes to perform a play.
Safety curtain	See **Iron.**
Scenes	In literary terms, a sub-division of an Act (q.v.). Continental stage usage indicates a new scene every time a character leaves the stage or a new one appears. In English and American practice a change of scene is only indicated when a particular course of action is complete or a new setting is called for within an Act.
Shutters	Late seventeenth-century term for pairs of large rectangular stage-flats (q.v.) which part or come together. When closed they acted as a backing for the scene played in front of them and when opened extended the scene either to the back of the stage or to a second pair of closed shutters. Shutters fell into disuse with the advent of three-dimensional scenery in the nineteenth century.
Slips	Side seats in a theatre at circle or gallery level and close to the stage. They are usually parallel with the side walls of the auditorium.
SM	Stage manager.
Son-et-lumière	An open-air sound and light show featuring a historic building. Such shows do not have actors but use their recorded voices. Constantly changing coloured lighting effects (behind different windows or on different parts of the building), music and snippets of recorded dialogue, together with a commentary, dramatise on site the story of some famous building and the events which took place there.
Stage directions	The acting area of a stage is *theoretically* divided into a grid pattern, each square being identified by a particular term. This enables actors to interpret a director's instructions when he is 'blocking' (q.v.) a play. The 'left' and 'right' designations always apply to the actors's left or right as he faces out front.

Street theatre   As the term implies, this is when actors take to the streets and the open air. Although much of street theatre is fun theatre, a great deal of it is also political theatre.

Strike   The term used when a piece of scenery or furniture has to be removed from the stage, e.g. 'Strike that chair.' When a complete set is 'struck', it is dismantled and removed leaving a bare stage.

Studio theatre   Implies a production/building which is intimate, in the sense that it is a small-scale production in a small hall or large room. Often a theatre's second small auditorium is called its studio theatre. Such studios generally have an uncluttered open-floor space with no fixed stage and little or no fixed seating. They are particularly suited to experimental work.

Stylised drama   Plays written and performed according to certain rules – resulting in an accentuated, non-naturalistic style, i.e. the language may be of a particular kind, the acting characterised by a specific uniform approach, with sets and costumes to match.

Symbolic   A production or performance is symbolic if it stands for, or denotes something else – not by exact representation but by vague suggestion, i.e. the morality figure *Everyman* is symbolic of the whole human race. Props (q.v.) can also be symbolic, e.g. a crown or throne standing for absolute power.

Symbolism   The practice of representing things by symbols. Chekhov's cherry orchard represents many things – an outdated past, the Russian serfs, an unproductive useless group of people, etc. Maeterlinck is the most famous symbolist playwright, but there are elements of symbolism in the work of Ibsen, Strindberg, W. B. Yeats, Synge and Chekhov.

Tabs   The main stage curtain, also called 'House-tabs'. Tab is an abbreviation of *tableau*, a popular nineteenth-century theatre practice of 'freezing the action' at the end of an Act, on which the curtain fell. It then rose again to reveal the *tableau vivant*.

Tech. run	Technical rehearsal or run-through of a play in which the actors are absent and only the technical areas of lighting, sound and effects are rehearsed.
Tormentors	Huge pieces of scenery, usually rectangular flats (q.v.), painted black or covered in black velvet or cloth, placed either side of the stage just inside the proscenium arch to narrow down the stage opening.
Trap	Short for trapdoor, which is cut into the stage floor or a flat (q.v.), to allow the sudden appearance or disappearance of an actor.
Try out	A production is 'tried out' in the provinces before it is brought into the West End of London. Today largely superseded by previews (q.v.).
Up-stage	That part of the stage furthest away from the audience. The term is derived from the perspective stage of the fifteenth-century Italian theatre which used a raked stage. The rake was particularly steep towards the back of the stage – hence *up*-stage.
Wings	The areas on either side of the stage not visible to an audience, in which the cast stand when about to make an entrance on stage. The term is also applied to *wing flats* (q.v.) or *wing drapes,* placed on either side of the stage to mask off the wings.
Workshop	Workshop theatre implies work in progress. Rehearsals are conducted in front of an invited audience who may also be invited to criticize or contribute. The term also covers the sort of activity undertaken by drama-in-education teams for audiences of schoolchildren. Such workshops are devoted to the comprehension and demonstration of a play – often a local examination text.

suggestions for further reading

Greek theatre

Kitto, H. D. F.: *The Greeks.* Pelican
Kitto, H. D. F.: *Greek Tragedy.* University Paperbacks No. 140
The plays are available in Penguin.

Roman theatre

Beare, W.: *The Roman Stage.* University Paperbacks No. 238
The plays are available in Penguin.

Medieval theatre

Axton, Richard: *European Drama of the Early Middle Ages.*
    Hutchinson University Library
Kahrl, J. Stanley: *Traditions of Medieval English Drama.*
    Hutchinson University Library
Tydeman, W.: *The Theatre in the Middle Ages.* Cambridge
    University Press
English Mystery Plays, Morality Plays, and Tudor Interludes
    are available in Penguin.

Elizabethan theatre

Bradbrook, M. C.: *The Growth and Structure of Elizabethan
    Comedy.* Peregrine

Bradbrook, M. C.: *Themes and Conventions of Elizabethan Tragedy.* Cambridge University Press

Brown, J. R. and Harris, B. (eds.): *Elizabethan Theatre.* No. 9 in Stratford-Upon-Avon Studies. Edward Arnold

Gurr, Andrew: *The Shakespearean Stage 1574–1642.* Cambridge University Press

Gorley Putt, S.: *The Golden Age of English Drama.* Brewer & Rowman and Littlefield, Cambridge

Hattaway, Michael: *Elizabethan Popular Theatre.* Routledge & Kegan Paul

Shakespeare

Burgess, Anthony: *Shakespeare.* Penguin

Ford, Boris (ed.): *The Age of Shakespeare.* Pelican Guide to English Literature (Vol. 2)

Muir, K. and Schoenbaum, S.: *A New Companion to Shakespeare Studies.* Cambridge University Press

Reese, M. M.: *Shakespeare His World and His Work.* Revised edition. Edward Arnold

Wain, John: *The Living World of Shakespeare.* Macmillan

Traversi, Derek: *An Approach to Shakespeare* 2nd. revision. New York

See also the *Casebook Series* for each individual play published by Macmillan.

Jacobean and Caroline theatre

Bamborough, J. B.: *Ben Jonson.* Hutchinson University Library

Brown, J. R. and Harris, B. (eds.) *Jacobean Theatre.* Stratford-Upon-Avon Studies No. 1. Edward Arnold

Ellis-Fermor, Una: *The Jacobean Drama.* University Paperbacks No. 143

Knights, L. C.: *Drama and Society in the Age of Jonson.* Chatto & Windus

Ornstein, Robert: *The Moral Vision of Jacobean Tragedy.* Madison, New York

Plays of the period (Elizabethan to Caroline) are available in paperback singly or in collections published by Penguin, New Mermaids series, Regents Renaissance Drama series, Everyman's University Library, Oxford University Press, Edward Arnold.

Restoration theatre

Avery, Emmett L. and Scouten, Arthur H.: *The London Stage 1660–1700.* Southern Illinois University Press

Holland, Norman N.: *The First Modern Comedies.* Indiana University Press

Hotson, L.: *The Commonwealth and Restoration Stage.* Harvard University Press

Loftis, John (ed.): *Restoration Drama.* Modern Essays in Criticism series, Oxford University Press

Summers, Montague: *The Restoration Theatre.* New York

The plays are readily available in paperback in Regents Restoration Drama series, Penguin, the New Mermaids Series, Oxford University Press.

eighteenth- and nineteenth-century theatre

Booth, Michael R.: *Victorian Spectacular Theatre 1850–1910.* Routledge & Kegan Paul

Nicoll, Allardyce: *The Garrick Stage.* Manchester University Press

Nicoll, Allardyce: *Late Nineteenth Century Drama* (two volumes). Cambridge University Press

Rowell, George: *The Victorian Theatre.* Clarendon Press, Oxford.

Southern, Richard: *The Victorian Theatre: a pictorial survey.* David & Charles

Play collections are available in Oxford University Press (old *World's Classic* series), Macmillan Modern Dramatists series, J. M. Dent & Sons.

twentieth-century theatre

Billington, Michael: *The Modern Actor.* Hamilton

Brook, Peter: *The Empty Space.* Pelican

Brustein, Robert: *The Theatre of Revolt*. Methuen

Elsom, John: *Post-War British Theatre*. Revised edition.
    Routledge & Kegan Paul

Esslin, Martin: *The Theatre of the Absurd*. Penguin

Findlater, Richard: *The Unholy Trade*. London

Hayman, Ronald: *Set up: An anatomy of the English theatre
    today*. Eyre Methuen

Hinchliffe, Arnold: *British Theatre 1950–70*. Blackwell

Marshall, Norman: *The Other Theatre*. London

Taylor, J. R.: *Anger and After*. Methuen

Taylor, J. R.: *The Rise and Fall of the Well-Made Play*. Methuen

Trewin, J. C.: *The Edwardian Theatre*. Blackwell

Trewin, J. C.: *Theatre in the Twenties*. London

Trewin, J. C.: *Theatre in the Thirties*. London

general surveys

Cameron, K. M. and Hoffman, T. J. C.: *A Guide to Theatre
    Study* (mainly American Theatre). 2nd. edition.
    Macmillan, New York

Craik, T. W. (gen. ed.): *The Revels History of Drama in English*
    (Vols. I–VII). Methuen

Forbes, Bryan: *That Despicable Race* (A History of the British
    Acting Tradition). Elm Tree Books

Gascoigne, Bamber: *World Theatre*. Ebury Press

Hartnoll, Phyllis: *The Oxford Companion to the Theatre*

Leacroft, Richard: *The Development of the English Playhouse*.
    Eyre Methuen

Nagler, A. M.: *A Source Book in Theatrical History*.
    Dover Publications Inc., New York

Nicoll, Allardyce: *The Development of the Theatre*. London

Southern, Richard: *Changeable Scenery*. Faber & Faber

Taylor, J. R.: *The Penguin Dictionary of the Theatre*

Wickham, Glynne: *Early English Stages 1300 to 1660*
    (Vols. I & II Parts I and II). Routledge & Kegan Paul

Many of these books will not be readily available in a local
bookshop but can be obtained through the public library.

index

Picture Credits

BBC Hulton Picture Library 139; John Vere Brown *frontis.*, 156; Bush Theatre (Jane Harper) 151; Nobby Clark 6, 17, 22; Joe Cocks 25, 38 and 39; Donald Cooper 154; Chris Davis/Network 41, 52; Gus de Cozar 73; Zoë Dominic 90, 99, 127; Eyre Methuen (from *The Development of the English Playhouse* by Richard Leacroft) 165; John Haynes 160; The Lyric Theatre, Hammersmith 164; The Raymond Mander and Joe Mitchenson Theatre Collection 36, 134, 141, 142; The Mansell Collection 74, 93, 103, 109, 112; The Royal Exchange Theatre, Manchester 119, 168; The Royal Shakespeare Company (David Farrell) 157; Reg Wilson 14, 63.